A basic textile book

Weaving on card showing strong textural interest. Dried flower heads, seedpods, braids, cut fabric, cotton and sisal were used freely to create contrasting areas of texture

Margaret Seagroatt

A basic textile book

VNR VAN NOSTRAND REINHOLD COMPANY
New York   Cincinnati   Toronto

Acknowledgements

Acknowledgements and thanks to Brian Hill for the frontispiece photograph; The Wool Marketing Board for figs 1, 2 and 3; Lullingstone Silk Farm for fig. 4; The International Institute for Cotton for fig 5; Lambeg Industrial Research Association for fig 6; the Association of Jute Spinners and Manufacturers for fig 7; Jim Roberts for figs 25, 28, 31, 75-9; Frank McGonigal for all the other photographs; Ann Sutton, in whose courses at Barry Summer School I first encountered the creative possibilities of knitting and crochet; the children of Dovecot Infants School, their headmistress Mrs Richards and their teacher Mrs Ann Russell (my daughter), for their co-operation; and all my former students.

Copyright © 1975 by Margaret Seagroatt
Library of Congress Catalog Card Number 75–12165
ISBN: 0 442-25064-9 cloth
ISBN: 0 442-25066-5 paper

This book was designed and produced by
The Herbert Press Ltd, London, England
Printed in Great Britain by Jolly & Barber Ltd, Rugby

Published in 1975 by Van Nostrand Reinhold Company
A Division of Litton Educational Publishing, Inc.
450 West 33rd Street, New York, NY 10001, U.S.A.

Van Nostrand Reinhold Limited
1410 Birchmount Road, Scarborough, Ontario M1P 2E7, Canada

16 15 14 13 12 11 10 9 8 7 6 5 4 3 2 1

Library of Congress Cataloging in Publication Data

Seagroatt, Margaret.
　A basic textile book

　Bibliography: p.
　　1. Hand spinning.　　2. Hand weaving.　　3. Dyes
and dyeing – Textile fibers.　　I. Title.
TT847.S4　1975　　　746.1　　　75-12165
ISBN 0-442-25064-9
ISBN 0-442-25066-5 pbk.

Contents

Introduction

We live in a sophisticated society in which most of our basic needs are catered for by mass-production. This is especially so in the field of textiles, where we rarely, if ever, see the raw materials spun into yarn, or the yarn woven into cloth. This book has evolved in response to requests from students being trained as teachers. Short courses were given at their college in which the basic elements of spinning, weaving and dyeing were explored in a way which encouraged creative exercises that could be practised at home or in the classroom; and, inevitably, I was asked if there was a book about it. 'Yes', they would say, when presented with a booklist, 'but isn't there just *one* book?' It transpired that what was needed was a book which left off where most books on textiles start. Thinking about this, I realised that there must be a number of people who would enjoy working in the medium if they felt that the process was within their capabilities, and, moreover, did not cost too much, at least at first. In other words, the need was for a book about beginning the various aspects of work with textiles, so that the more advanced books could be more readily understood. So this book was devised, not only for students and teachers, but for ordinary people who have neither money nor space to embark on anything too ambitious, but who would like to explore the various textile possibilities. Most of the simple ideas have been evolved from a study of weaving, spinning and the dyeing of fabrics in primitive countries, and a feeling for the qualities of the basic materials. The initial information on fibres is an essential introduction to the practice of any of the textile crafts, for the finished article depends on the behaviour of the fibres of which it is composed. Although the equipment recommended is simple, the work produced on it may very well achieve a very high standard.

I hope that from these beginnings the reader will be led to acquire more complex skills, either in part-time classes (local authorities in the UK may be able to supply a class in their area if enough people demand it), or by further reading.

This book would not have been possible without the work of many students, and without the lively discussions that were part of it. To all these students, and particularly those at the now defunct Kirkby Fields College, Liverpool, I give my acknowledgements and thanks.

1 Fibres

Fabrics are made from yarns which are made from fibres. The natural fibres are of animal, vegetable and mineral origin.

Natural fibres
Animal Mainly wool and hair, chiefly sheep, camel, alpaca, vicuna, mohair and cashmere, with marginal use of cow, horse, goat and rabbit. Silk.
Vegetable From seeds, stems and leaves; the main fibres are cotton, flax, hemp, jute, ramie and sisal, the minor fibres including coir, raffia etc.
Mineral Asbestos is the only mineral fibre.

Synthetic fibres
These are divided into two main groups: the regenerated fibres, which have a natural basis of cellulose; and the man-made fibres, of chemical origin.
Regenerated Rayons, protein fibres.
Man-made Nylon, Terylene, Orlon, Acrilan, Dacron, Courtelle, etc. Glass fibre. There are many types of man-made fibre, all of a different character but all made in a similar way.

Animal fibres
Sheep
The sheep is the universally domesticated animal which produces a unique fibre capable of being made into a yarn. It has its origin in pre-history, when its ancestors, the Argali, the Mouflon and the Bighorn, roamed Central Asia, Europe and North America. These breeds are still to be found in remote places – the Argali in Siberia and Tibet, the Mouflon in Cyprus and Sardinia, and the Bighorn in the north-western part of the North American continent. The Mouflon has a silky fleece, its most typical descendant being the Merino. Most European breeds are descended from the Mouflon, while the British breeds, which are markedly more woolly, have strong infusions of Argali from early in the Stone Age. Sheep were domesticated from very early times in Central Asia, and when man was driven into Europe by the oncoming Ice Age he took his Argali flocks to be interbred with the Mouflon.

British sheep, from which many of the world's present-day breeds originate, are of three main types: the *Down Breeds* or *Shortwools*, which live in the warm, dry, south-eastern parts of the country; the *Longwools*, which thrive in wetter regions with rich pastures; and the *Mountain Breeds*, which exist on exposed hills and uplands. Their fleeces seem to take on the characteristics of the land which feeds them, and if a sheep is taken away from its natural habitat its

1 A typical Southdown sheep

fleece will alter in character; the poorer the pasture, the finer the wool. In each main type of fleece there are many breeds, each differing in character and used for different purposes, which has an important bearing on the type of fleece used for spinning.

The *Shortwools* are usually associated with chalky uplands which are covered with short grass. The appearance of these breeds is characteristic, with short, dense fleece standing out from the body to give it a rounded shape much beloved by illustrators of children's books. In this group the best known is the Southdown (fig. 1), which grows the shortest and finest wool with a staple length of 1·5–10 cm (½–4 ins). It is crisp in handle, non-lustrous, pure white, very elastic and soft; the yarn spun from it is used in light clothing materials. The Southdown is the forerunner of all the other Down breeds. The Shropshire, a very old breed, is found in the Longmynd area and is related to the Welsh Mountain breed. It is larger than the Southdown, and the fleece can weigh up to 8 kilos (18 lbs) in contrast to the Southdown's 2 kilos (4 lbs). Other Shortwools include the Suffolk, Hampshire, Dorset and Oxford Downs, the Dorset and Wiltshire Horns, the Ryeland from Herefordshire, and the Devon Closewool. The Wiltshire Horn is the only sheep without fleece; it is a very large animal with a wiry coat, which moults like a dog, and is bred for meat. All the fleeces in this group are used for fine woollen fabrics and some light tweeds.

An intermediate type of sheep is bred on the borders of England and Wales. The Kerry Hill, Clun Forest and Radnor all have a

2　A Blackface ewe and lamb. Note the long guard hairs on the mother

common origin in either the Welsh Mountain or the Shropshire Down, and are used extensively in the manufacture of wools for the Welsh woollen industry, to be used for hosiery, knitting yarns, flannels, blankets, felts and fine tweeds.

The *Mountain Breeds* have a coarse, medium-length staple, and are used for hard-wearing coarse tweeds and for carpet yarns. The Welsh Mountain is the least typical with much finer wool than the others, giving Welsh wool its characteristic softness which is, nevertheless, combined with hardwearing quality. This fleece, with its medium staple and soft but firm handle, is used in the Welsh mills for bedcovers, knitted goods and clothing fabrics. It is ideal for first attempts at hand spinning. Wool from the Scotch Blackface is used extensively in the carpet trade and for coarse tweeds, the fleece being resilient and hairy (fig. 2). The long hairs on the surface of the fleece are composed of kemp, or hollow hairs, which do not take dye, and these protect the sheep from weather and burrs; they also give Harris tweed its characteristic appearance, a blurred and hairy surface interspersed with white. The Herdwick is the hardiest mountain breed, inhabiting the bleak hills and fells of the Lake District, and is possibly Scandinavian in origin. Its fleece is softer than that of the Blackface, varying in colour from white through brown to black, and is used for tweeds and carpet yarns. Other mountain breeds include the Swaledale from Yorkshire, the Lonk from the northern Pennines, and the Derbyshire Gritstone. The Cheviot is an important breed, the result of crossing an indigenous breed with

Merinos imported from Spain in the 15th century. The fleece is dense and woolly, growing longer in the lowlands than on the higher hills, and softer than that of other mountain breeds. It is used for Cheviot tweeds and for blankets, hosiery and fancy worsteds. West of England tweeds are made from the fleece of the Exmoor Horn, which inhabits the Devon and Somerset moors. It is another ancient breed, very hardy, and its wool is short, soft and fine.

The *Longwools* have a long, lustrous, curly or wavy fleece which is used in the worsted trade because of these characteristics. The most important breed is the Leicester (fig. 3), found in the Midlands and other areas and used extensively in cross-breeding. Robert Bakewell improved the breed in the 18th century, and it now produces mutton as well as wool. The Border Leicester, a cross between Leicester and Cheviot and now an important breed, is kept on the Lancashire and Cumberland fells and used for crossing with Swaledale, Blackface and Suffolk. It is hardy and adaptable, with a wavy, silky fleece. The Lincoln, largest of the British sheep, with a very long and wavy fleece which has been known to reach a length of 80 cm (32 ins) at its first clip, is also used extensively for cross-breeding and is found throughout the world. The Cotswold, bred since the 15th century in the Cotswold Hills, the Chilterns and Dorset, has a white fleece similar to the Leicester. Other longwools are the Dartmoor and Devon Long-wools and the Romney Marsh. The latter has the softest of the Longwool fleeces and is a pure strain due to the isolation of its habitat; it has been exported to New Zealand and South America.

In addition to these three types of British breed, there is the soft, fine-fleeced Shetland from the islands north of Scotland; the Jacob, from Dorset, thought to be of Mediterranean origin, which has a fine, black and white piebald fleece; the brown Loghtan from the Isle of Man, with two sets of horns; and the St Kilda and Soay, the half-wild sheep found in the islands of that name. Some of these breeds are now being preserved in special parks.

The thirty-odd breeds of British sheep are the result of careful selective breeding, for both meat and wool, and have been used widely throughout the world for cross-breeding, producing other breeds, such as the New Zealand Corriedale, which are now typical of their particular habitat and requirements.

The most important sheep apart from the British breeds is the Merino. This was originally a Spanish breed and was imported into Australia in 1790. It has a soft, dense, silky fleece which grows in the many folds of skin produced by careful breeding in order to present the maximum area on which wool can grow. It flourishes on poor land, and has been bred for wool rather than meat; it is also extensively cross-bred with other breeds to alter the quality of the wool. The fleece is used for a variety of purposes in the woollen industry.

3 A Leicester Longwool sheep

The other breeds found in Australia have been bred from British Longwools crossed with Merino and Rambouillet (see below), producing wool which is both strong and fine. The chief sheep districts are in the south, east and west of Australia, the wools from Victoria, New South Wales, Queensland and South and West Australia all having different qualities and characteristics.

New Zealand is also an important wool producing country. The climate is similar to that of Great Britain, and the sheep are derived from the selective interbreeding of British varieties with Merino.

African wools come chiefly from the southern part of the continent and are of two types, the Merino with its soft, fine wool contrasting with that of the native Cape sheep which is much coarser. North African wools are a cross between Merino and the indigenous sheep, and vary in coarseness according to the proportion of Merino in the cross.

The Rambouillet is almost pure Merino, imported into France in 1785. Exported to America in 1840, it is now a very important factor in the production of distinctive breeds in the USA and South America, combined with a variety of British breeds. An indigenous American sheep, the Rocky Mountain, is descended from the Bighorn, and is found in the high lands of the west. South America, particularly the Argentine, is a very important wool growing area, its sheep being descended from the crossing of Merino or Rambouillet with British breeds.

There are many other wool producing areas of the world. A great variety of sheep breeds are found in the Asian countries, from the wools of Baghdad and Bokhara, used in carpets, to the Marco Polo sheep from the high wild parts of Central Asia and the fat-tailed, long-eared sheep found in India.

Wool fibre

The structure of the wool fibre, which is a protein, is made up of three layers. The *medulla* is the central part containing large round cells; these are more marked in coarse fibres and in kemp, the dead, brittle hairs which are filled with air, and are almost absent in the finer types of wool. The *cortex* is the main part of the fibre containing the pigment in long spindle-shaped cells. The *epidermis* is the outer layer of overlapping, horny scales, the edges of which project from root to tip of the fibre. It is the epidermis which gives wool its inimitable character and explains why 'there is no substitute for wool'. Finer wools, with more scales per inch, have a low lustre, and the large number of scales entangle easily to give a good spinning property. The scale formation also leads to a good felting property. Longwools have comparatively fewer, but larger, scales and are therefore more lustrous but do not felt easily. Felting, caused by the entanglement of the scales, is used to thicken cloth and obscure the weave, as in the manufacture of blazer cloths. Anti-shrink processes modify the scales by various chemical means, so that felting is made more difficult. Another characteristic of wool is its crimp, or wave, more marked in the Down breeds and Merino. Raw wool may contain as much as twenty per cent grease, which is exuded from the animal's skin and left in the fibre. This is removed before spinning and, in its refined form as lanolin, goes to make lipsticks and ointments.

Wool has three important properties, all due to its inherent structure, which are difficult to imitate in a synthetic fibre: 1. It is very elastic, the Shortwools being more so than the Longwools; this is important in clothing, as the fibre regains its shape when stretched. 2. It is a resilient fibre, springing back into place when crushed; this is most apparent in the Longwools used in carpet manufacture. 3. The fibre will hold moisture up to thirty per cent of its own weight without feeling wet, and gives off heat when moist, which is why woollen garments are held in such high regard in cold, wet, mountainous regions.

Other wools

The other wools and hairs which grow on animals are different from sheep's wool in that the scale formation does not allow most of them to felt as easily. Mohair, which comes from the half-wild Angora goat, a native of Turkey, is now also grown in the USA and Africa and is the most important hair fibre. The fibres, which are white, long, lustrous and very resilient have a staple length of 15–30 cm (6–12 in), and spin into a strong, smooth yarn which does not felt. It is used in fashion fabrics and knitwear, also for velvets and pile upholstery, and linings. The Llama and Alpaca belong to the camel family and live in Peru. The hair is similar to mohair, and to a Leicester wool, with a staple length of about 30 cm (12 in) and in a variety of natural shades from whites through browns to black. It is unbleachable, which limits its industrial use, and the coat weighs only 1½ kilos (3 lbs) per clip and is shorn only every other year, so it is usually used for jackets and linings in its natural colour. The undercoat of the Camel, the two-humped kind from Tibet, is very light and has special heat-insulating properties. It separates easily from the coarse outer coat, and is used in its natural brownish colour for coats and dressing gowns. The coarse strong outer coat, which has a 25 cm (10 in) staple compared with the 5 cm (2 in) inner coat, is used for beltings, braids, etc. The Vicuna is also from the high Andean plains of Peru and produces the finest and most expensive wool in the world, which was once exclusive to the Inca royalty. Very wild, depending on speed for survival, it was once shot for its coat, which even then produced only four ounces of the fine inner hair every two years. It is now protected though not domesticated, and rounded up in order to secure the fleece. This has great lustre, strength and beauty in addition to fineness, and is used in its natural golden-brown colour. Research is taking place in cross-breeding with the Alpaca, producing a Paco-vicuna which combines the fineness of the Vicuna with the longer and more plentiful fibres of the Alpaca. The fibre is made into a luxury cloth for coats and jackets. The Cashmere or Tibetan goat from Central Asia produces another expensive wool. The undercoat which, again, only grows four ounces a year, is removed by combing; it is very soft and fine, and needs special carding machinery to separate it from the outer coat. This very beautiful yarn is used for fashion garments and luxury knitwear and also, traditionally, for Cashmere and Paisley shawls. Cow, horse and goat hairs play a small part in the textile scene, cow and goat hair being combined with wool for rugs and upholstery in Scandinavia, and also used elsewhere for mats. Horsehair is used in upholstery, and has a somewhat strange use in the manufacture of gloves used to groom greyhounds. Fur from the rabbit, both common and Angora, and from the musquash, squirrel and beaver are occasionally used to give a special quality to a blend of wool and hair, usually in light tweeds.

Silk

The Chinese recorded the cultivation of silk, or sericulture (derived from the original Chinese word), as long ago as 2640 BC, and its romantic origins are retold in myth and legend. A Chinese princess, Si-ling-chi, was said to have watched a silkworm making its cocoon and, realising that the silk thread could be unwound, learned how to rear the silkworms. This was the beginning of an industry that flourished exclusively in China for the unbelievable span of 3000 years; the secrets of its manufacture were strictly kept, for revealing them invoked the death penalty. It was not until AD 300 that the secret was revealed, some say by the kidnapping of workers, to Korea, then to Japan. A Chinese princess who married an Indian prince smuggled some eggs and mulberry seeds out of China to Khotan in AD 419, thus spreading sericulture into the rest of Asia. The silk cloth was exported into Europe, but it was a luxury fabric and, being a monopoly of the Byzantine emperors, very expensive. The Emperor Justinian, in about AD 550, bribed two Persian monks who had lived as missionaries in China to bring some eggs back to Europe, which they did by hiding the eggs in their hollow bamboo staffs. The hatching of these eggs became the birth of a European silk industry which has been a source of wealth for well over a thousand years.

Silk comes from the larvae of the mulberry silkworm, *bombyx mori*, which is reared indoors. There are roughly 80 different types of moth which produce silk, though most of these are not suitable for commercial production. The wild silkworm, which feeds on oak leaves, castor oil plants, etc., produces Tussah and Eri silk, but the rearing of this cannot be controlled in the same way as *bombyx mori*. The eggs are specially selected to be disease-free, and rearing begins as soon as the leaves appear on the mulberry trees. The eggs, which have been stored during the winter in a cool place, are then warmed artificially (or, in peasant communities, by contact with the human skin, being placed in bags inside the warm cotton padded jackets worn by the Chinese). The eggs are spread on trays in an incubator, and within thirty days they hatch tiny black, hairy caterpillars 3 mm long. These are covered with perforated paper sprinkled with chopped mulberry leaves and the worms climb up through the perforations and start eating. The silkworm is a sensitive, choosy creature, and the leaves must be just right; fresh, slightly wilted, but not too much or the worm will refuse to eat. Once started on a constant supply of leaves, the worm literally eats until it bursts! It moults four times, and in about five weeks is over 8 cm (3 ins) long and ten thousand times heavier, being bloated with liquid silk and pale green in colour. Looking for somewhere to spin, it rears up and looks around for a place to secure its cocoon. Bundles of straw or bamboo twigs are placed ready, and the silkworm climbs up these before covering itself with silk (fig. 4). The liquid silk is contained in two glands, which emerge behind its head in a single tube called a spinneret, the liquid hardening into two filaments stuck together by a gummy substance called serecin which comes from another gland. The silkworm moves its head in a figure-of-eight motion, exuding the silk, which gradually covers its body, taking three days to form a cocoon. The silkworm shrinks in the process of exuding its silk and changes into a pupa and then a moth. In captivity the pupa is killed inside the cocoon by subjecting it to heat, to avoid breaking the

4 The silkworm
starting to spin

continuous filament of silk, but wild silk worms bite their way
through the end of the cocoon. If the worms are feeding on oak
leaves, as the Tussah variety does, the tannin makes the silk a pale
brown colour. There is about one mile of silk in the cocoon, but less
than half of this is usable in filament form, as the centre of the
filament is thicker than the two ends. The cocoons are placed in
hot water to soften the serecin, and stirred either with twigs or
revolving brushes until the ends of the silk filaments are caught
up, five or so at a time. These filaments are given a slight twist,
then reeled, and finally twisted to make a yarn. The waste silk left
from this process is carded and spun, as are the short fibres of the
wild varieties. The serecin is boiled off either in the yarn state, or
after weaving.

Silk is the longest natural textile fibre, and has the highest
strength for its cross section. It is fine, lustrous and elastic, and
more cloth may be made from a pound of silk than from any other
natural fibre. In addition, silk fibre has great beauty, not only in
appearance and texture but also in the sound it makes in
movement. Japan is an important producer and exporter, though
the best silk now comes from Italy. It is also produced in China,
India, France and Switzerland, and even to a limited extent in
England, where the Lullingstone Silk Farm has produced the silk
for velvet garments for royal occasions. It has always been
associated with royalty, high rank and luxury, and although its
use has been strongly challenged by the synthetic fibres, it is still
one of the important natural fibres in the fashion trade. Some
Eastern carpets, traditionally made of silk, still use it, sometimes
now in combination with wool.

Vegetable fibres

Cotton

This is the most important vegetable fibre; its use goes back to 3000 BC in India and possibly even to 12,000 BC in Egypt, and was refined until, by the 17th century, muslins spun on a handle spindle, so fine and light that 60 square metres (73 square yards) weighed only 500 grammes (1 lb), were being made at Dacca in India. This was far finer than the modern equivalent. Its use spread to the Mediterranean, and from there into Europe, the British East India Company being formed in 1600 and growing in influence, while at the same time cotton was being developed in the New World. By the time the Industrial Revolution was on its way a flourishing cotton trade existed, and became an important part of a world-wide textile industry.

The cotton fibre (fig 5) grows on the plant *gossypium*, a member of the mallow family, thriving in a sub-tropical climate. The bush has yellow flowers which drop to reveal a small seed pod called a boll, containing the seeds round which the cotton fibres grow. After about fifty days, when the boll can no longer contain the compressed fibres, it bursts open and the cotton bulges out. The boll should be picked immediately it opens. Although there are mechanical pickers, they are rather like huge vacuum cleaners into which bolls, leaves, twigs and dirt are drawn indiscriminately. Much of the picking, therefore, is still done by hand, several times in a season. The seeds are removed by a process of separation called ginning, and the cotton is then packed into bales, ready for spinning when it reaches its destination. The short fibres, or linters, removed by the first ginning, still adhere to the seeds, and these are subjected to a second ginning; the linters are used as a source of cellulose for the rayon industry; the seeds are crushed to extract the oil which is used for soap etc. and the residue is made into cattle cake.

The cotton fibre is made up of three parts: the outer cuticle containing deposits of cellulose and wax; the inner wall, the main part of the fibre containing pure cellulose; and the cell contents, or lumen, forming the central part of the fibre. As it grows the fibre is compressed and distorted. When the boll opens and the fibre dries, these distortions are fixed, and the fibre twists or convolutes, which helps its spinning properties. Because the cellulose is formed in minute threads, or fibrils, the fibre is porous and can readily absorb moisture, becoming stronger in the process. This is one of the most important properties of the cotton fibre. The fibres vary in length from 1·5 to 5 cm ($\frac{1}{2}$–2 in), the longest and finest Sea Island cotton coming from the West Indies, followed by the silky Egyptian fibre. Most of the medium staple is grown in the USA, and the coarser, short staple comes from India and China. Both medium and short staple cotton is grown in the USSR, and its cultivation is now a major industry in over sixty countries.

Cotton spinning machinery is so complex that a mill may only be

5 A cotton plant showing seedpod, flower and opened boll

equipped to spin one staple length. The length and fineness varies on the same type of cotton and even in the hairs on one seed, as well as from different bolls, plants and fields. As uniformity is important for spinning, the development of pure seed strains and the careful planning of planting are practised to lessen the variation. Unfavourable weather, disease and pests, notably the boll weevil, can prevent the fibre walls thickening properly so that the fibre cannot be spun easily. The thin immature fibres roll up and form neps, or tangles, in the yarn, and this makes it more difficult to dye.

Lancashire was an ideal place for the early development of cotton spinning because of its humid climate and plentiful supplies of coal and water. Humidity can now be artificially controlled in cotton mills, and the manufacture of cotton is now well-established in major countries throughout the world, with Britain and the USA the largest producers.

Other seed fibres in use include Tree Cotton, a weaker version of normal cotton, used for wadding; Kapok, which is similar, but very buoyant and used for stuffing upholstery and lifebelts; and the nut fibre Coir, from the coarse outer covering of the coconut, used for brushes, matting, ropes and twines.

Linen

Linen is thought to be the oldest plant fibre in the world to be used as a yarn. This is surprising as the fibre lies hidden within the woody stem, and is not immediately visible. Linen has been found in the pre-historic Swiss Lake Dwellings, and its use has been recorded in Egypt from 4500 BC, and probably goes back to an even earlier date. Ancient Egypt was the centre of flax production; the priests dressed in white linen robes, a symbol of religious purity which has continued in use for the robes of Roman Catholic priests. From the Mediterranean its cultivation spread all over

17

Europe into England, and particularly into Scotland and Ireland, where it became, and to a certain extent still is, an important industry. Linen was Europe's most important vegetable textile fibre until the 18th century, when Arkwright invented his machine for spinning a strong cotton thread, but in recent years it has declined in importance, although a great deal is still grown.

Linen comes from the flax plant, *Linum usistatissimum*, which produces a blue flower on a stem about 1 metre high. The stalks are slender, and are closely sown if grown for the fibre, but allowed to produce more flower by sowing further apart when grown for seed. When harvested by hand the plants are pulled up by the roots to avoid staining by the soil, and after being laid to dry for a few days they are ready for what is somewhat romantically called 'the long agony of flax' – the series of operations the fibre must undergo before it can become a yarn. The seeds and leaves are removed by *rippling* which involves drawing the heads through a comb, either by hand or mechanically. The crushed seed yields linseed oil, the residue goes to make cattle cake. Woody matter, pectins and cellular tissue hold the fibres together, and these are softened by *retting*, from an old Dutch word, *reten*, which means to rot. This may be done by dew retting, in which the flax is spread on the ground and left to rot naturally. It takes from four to eight weeks, and is a slow process, producing a poor quality grey fibre, but useful when no other water is available, as in parts of Russia. Dam retting may be done in dams or ponds dug near the growing area, and this takes about ten days. The flax has to be weighted down, or the gases produced would make it float. River retting is also practised, although it has now been forbidden because of pollution in Courtrai, in Belgium, where the best flax is grown. It has been superseded by tank retting in heated water, which only takes three days. The best fibre is produced by double retting, drying off between operations. A poorer fibre is produced in a few hours by chemical retting in caustic and acid solutions.

After drying the flax is subjected to *breaking*, which snaps the woody core into small pieces without damaging the fibre. Formerly it was beaten by hand, but fluted rollers are now employed for this process. *Scutching*, or *swingling* removes the snapped core and most of the bark, either by hand on a scutching board with a hinged handle which beats out the woody matter, or by machine. In former times scutching festivals were held in the villages, and the girls would work throughout one day in return for meals, until the work was finished. The waste from this process, called *shive*, is used for fuel, while the shorter fibres, or *tow*, are spun into coarse yarns. *Hackling* combs and separates the fibres by drawing them through pins set successively closer, providing another source of tow which is then carded again and twisted loosely into a sliver before dry spinning; the finer fibres are wetted in warm water before spinning, as this loosens the gums and makes a finer, smoother yarn.

Flax fibres lie in bundles embedded in pectinous gums between

6 The flax plant harvested mechanically

the bark and the core of the stem, and each bundle is made up of short fibres, called ultimates, again embedded in gums. Flax has strength, fineness, length and lustre, though it lacks elasticity. Its lustre and smooth appearance make is suitable for table linen, as the shine can be used to advantage in damask weaves. It conducts heat well, so is cool, though expensive, for sheets; it absorbs water, so is used for towels and glass cloths; its strength is used in good quality twines, rug warp and loom cord. Because the fibre is harder than cotton, dyestuffs do not penetrate so well and special techniques are used to ensure maximum absorption. It is processed to resist creasing, which is one of its characteristics. Because of the expense of its production, the use of flax has declined, but it is still used where a moisture resistant strength is required, as in sail and tent cloth, shoemakers' thread, bookbinders' twine, and fishing line. Scutching tow is used for sackcloth and rough ropes, combing tow for coarse linen, while the waste flax is used in bank notes, cigarette papers, and high grade paper. Most flax now comes from Russia, though it is not of good quality. The best comes from Courtrai, in Belgium, a pale straw colour which explains why blonde hair was described as 'flaxen'. Other good flaxes come from Ireland, Holland, and France. Egyptian flax is particularly long, while the Russian, Persian, Silesian and Austrian flaxes are weak.

Hemp

Hemp is also an ancient fibre, used in China in 2300 BC. Its use spread to Europe much later, appearing in Ancient Greece and Rome as rope, sailcloth and fishing nets. In the Middle Ages hempen garments were a sign of poverty, and it was then mainly used for ropes. It comes from the plant *cannabis sativa*, which grows to a height of $1\frac{1}{2}$–6 metres (5–20 feet). The male plants are grown only for the fibre, the female for fibre and seeds, which yield oil. The fibres ripen before the seed, so the male plants are sown

19

before the female. The harvester suffers from violent headaches from the stupefying smell given off by the plant, which is related to Indian hemp from which hashish is extracted. After retting, the fibre is subjected to the same complex series of operations as the flax fibre. Its structure is similar to flax but much coarser, and being unaffected by salt water it is used for good quality twines, ropes, cables, nets, tarpaulins, sailcloth and canvas, and also for rug warps, although finer Italian hemp can be used for table linens. It is grown all over the world; Russia produces half the total, Italy, Yugoslavia and the USA are also important producers.

Jute

Since prehistoric times jute has been used in India, mostly for cordage and coarse fabrics. The East India Company first recognised its possibilities, but it was not until after 1835 that jute could be spun satisfactorily by machine and the Dundee jute industry was developed. It comes from the stem of the plant *Corchorus*, and grows, like hemp and flax, between the bark and the core, the fibre bundles growing in concentric layers while the ultimates are very short. It is a much weaker fibre than the other two because of the shortness of the ultimates. The plant grows $2\frac{1}{2}$–5 metres (8–15 feet) high, and is retted in pools or rivers, the fibre being stripped while still in the water. It is hung on poles to dry and then sent to the mills in large bundles. It is softened with water or oil before spinning, as it is quite harsh. Yellow to brown in colour, it takes dye well, and is made into sacks, ropes, twines and backing for linoleums. The tow is used for upholstery, stuffing, roofing felts, and, after treatment with caustic soda which curls it, may be blended with wool to make cheap clothing fabrics. It is gradually

7 Jute harvesting in Bangladesh

being superseded by synthetic fibres, which are stronger and do not rot, and even its use in linoleums is dwindling as they are replaced by vinyl floor coverings which do not need backing. The political troubles in India and Pakistan, with their effect on the jute crop, are accelerating this process, but if there is to be a world shortage of petroleum, from which man-made fibres are derived, this may very well mean at least a partial return to natural fibres of all kinds.

Ramie, or China Grass

Ramie comes from the plant *Boehmeria*, which is related to the nettle. It was used in Mediterranean countries in early times, and some mummy wrappings from the pre-dynastic period 5000–3300 BC have been found in Egypt. It was also used by the early American Indians. It is now found in warm countries, including China, Japan, the USA, South America, the USSR and parts of Europe.

The plant grows 1–2 metres (4–6 feet) high and after harvesting is soaked in water, the fibre removed by a scraping process called decorticating. Knives made from bamboo and shell are used, as well as metal, the process varying in different areas. The fibre is white and lustrous, absorbs moisture well, is strong but inelastic, and takes dye well. It is used for canvas and packing materials, fishing nets and sewing threads, also for upholstery and clothing fabrics.

Leaf fibres
Sisal

This is the best known leaf fibre and comes from the fibrous veins forming the structure of the leaf of the plant *Agave sisalana*, which is grown in Central America. It was used by the Aztecs for threads, cords, cloth and paper; an intoxicating liquor was also fermented from the leaves. The Spaniards brought it to Europe after the conquest of Mexico, but it is now to be found mainly in East Africa.

The agave grows as a rosette, with fleshy leaves 1–2 metres (3–6 feet) long and a flower stalk up to 6 metres (20 feet) high. After flowering, buds are produced, which in turn become new plants which take about seven years to flower. The leaves, which contain the fibres, are cut and sent to a decorticator, a machine which scrapes, washes and separates the fibres. These are then dried and bleached by the sun. The waste, or flume tow, is spun into coarse yarn for sacks, and also produces wax, sugar and alcohol.

The fibre is stiff, strong and white and not very flexible. It dyes easily with direct or acid dyes, the natural lustre enhancing the colours. Commercially, it is used for ropes, twines, mattings, rugs and even ladies' hats. It is strong when spun, and its inflexible fibres both hold a shape as a spun yarn and acquire a delicacy of appearance as a fibre, making it ideal for all sorts of decorative three-dimensional bound forms as well as for woven structures.

Abaca, or Manila hemp

This does not come from Manila, neither is it hemp. It is a relation of the banana plant, called *Musa textilis*, and is grown extensively in the Philippines and, more recently, in Central America. Magellan saw textiles made of abaca during his global voyage in 1521. The plant can grow to over 7 metres (25 feet) and consists of a cluster of leaf stalks. These may be produced continuously for up to 30 years, each stalk being cut when it reaches an average diameter of 20 cm (8 ins). The fibres are then processed, either by decortication, or by separating the pulp from the fibres by scraping with a knife. The strips thus produced are called tuxies, which then have to be sorted for quality. The coarser grades are used for ropes and twines, having a natural lustre and being resistant to salt water. The finer grades are used for clothing, particularly for the crisp, silk-like, beautifully embroidered shirts worn by the Philippines. Other uses are in paper-making, hats, shoes, carpets, table-mats, etc.

New Zealand Flax

An indigenous New Zealand plant, which was first described by Captain Cook when he brought back his collection of costumes, now in the Pitt-Rivers Museum at Oxford. The plant, *Phormium tenax*, has long slender leaves containing the fibres, which are stripped, washed and dried in the sun. After scutching, the fibres are compressed into bales and used, mainly locally, for ropes, twines and coarse sackings, and formerly more extensively used in Maori costume.

Piassava

This fibre comes from the leaf stalks of a variety of palms. It is stiff and unbending, the fibres coming from the base of a leaf which is 20 feet long. They are retted, hackled, dried, bundled and trimmed, and are mainly used commercially for brooms and brushes in a variety of brown shades. The fibres, because of their stiffness, may be used for woven hangings, table-mats, mattings, etc. It is grown in Brazil and West Africa.

Raffia

This is obtained from the surface layer of skin from the young leaflets of the Piassava or other palms. The skin is cut into strips, and dried and baled. Raffia in its natural straw colour may be used for hats, for tying the garden plants, and for weaving and other handicrafts. It may be dyed with basic dyes, though the colours do not seem to be very fast. It comes mainly from Madagascar.

Pineapple

Called Caroa, and cultivated in Eastern countries, the Pacific Islands and the West Indies, the leaves of the pineapple yield a strong white fibre which makes cordage, the finer threads being made into a linen-like cloth. Experiments in rotting and scraping the leaves may be made with the small leaves from the fruits we buy; steeping the leaves in warm water in a screw-topped jar until they are soft will produce fibres strong enough to make a primitive thread; it will also produce a strong smell!

Mineral fibre
Asbestos
Strangely, this is an early fibre, having been mined since classical times; the name comes from the Greek word *asbestinon*, meaning inextinguishable. Chinese scribes used it for false sleeves from which the dirt could be burnt, and Pliny mentions it being used for shrouds for royal corpses, keeping their ashes separate from the rest of the pyre. He also tells of napkins being cleaned by burning after banquets. Charlemagne is also alleged to have used this trick upon the ambassadors of Haroun-al-Raschid and so confounded them that they advised their master not to attack such a powerful wizard. If this is true, the course of history may have been changed by a minor textile fibre! Asbestos is a rock which has crystallised in fibrous form, looking and feeling rather like wood. The fibres are closely packed, and a greenish-white colour. Pliny described it as being red and coming from India, although it was mined in Cyprus. It was also mined in Russia in the 18th century, but Canada is now its most important source. Asbestos is resistant to fire, and though it is difficult to spin, this property makes it an invaluable fibre where fire-resistance is needed. It is not strong, though durable, and is used for fireproof clothing, theatre curtains, electrical insulation, conveyor belting, packing and gaskets.

Synthetic fibres
The last hundred years have seen a rapidly increasing knowledge of the chemical construction of textile fibres. The fibres of natural origin consist of molecules which themselves are like threads, the atoms of which are in the form of a long thin chain. The properties of these fibres are derived from the constitution of their molecules, which lie along the length of the fibre in closely packed, linked bundles. It is the linkage and alignment of these bundles of molecules which give the fibres their varying properties of strength and flexibility. The properties of the natural fibres are controlled by the way they grow, and cannot be changed very much. A synthetic fibre, however, can be controlled.

All synthetic fibres are made in a similar way. A substance which will form a fibre is manufactured in bulk, with the molecules, still like minute threads, lying at random. The substance is then heated or dissolved, and forced, or extruded, through fine holes, emerging to harden into a filament. The molecules have then been stretched and aligned along the fibre, which is then further stretched to increase its cohesion and therefore its strength. The difference between the regenerated fibres and the truly synthetic, or man-made, fibres is that the former are derived from natural substances such as cotton, wood and milk, while the latter are made from simple chemical elements, petroleum, air and water. It is not within the scope of this book to describe them in detail, but the salient features of the most important types of fibre are given.

Regenerated fibres

Rayons The scientist, Robert Hooke, in his *Micrographia* published in 1664, suggested the possible imitation of the way a silkworm spins its thread. In 1754 de Réaumur suggested varnish as a suitable liquid; Keller in 1840 invented a process of dissolving wood pulp, while Schwabe, in Manchester, invented a machine for spinning a synthetic fibre, which, however, proved to be not very practical; Schoenbein followed in 1846 with his treatment of cellulose with nitric acid to make nitro-cellulose, which was not suitable for a textile fibre because it was explosive. All these had been unsuccessful attempts to dissolve natural cellulose. Audemars, in 1855, discovered that nitro-cellulose could be dissolved in a mixture of alcohol and ether, which evaporated when the sticky substance was drawn out on the point of a needle, but the fibres were still inflammable. In 1885 Sir Joseph Swan treated the filaments chemically, and changed them back to cellulose, but this was used for the filaments in electric light bulbs, and not for a textile fibre. Count Chardonnet, in France, after over ten years of experimenting, opened the first factory to produce what was then described as artificial silk in 1889. This was a shiny, somewhat cheap-looking fibre, and has now been superseded by the three rayons in commercial use today.

VISCOSE RAYON The British chemists Cross, Bevan and Beadle first developed the substance which was to be known as viscose rayon in 1895. Working independently in the USA, Arthur Little produced his version of viscose rayon in the same year. A sticky, or viscous, liquid was made by treating cellulose first with caustic soda, then with carbon disulphide, and then dissolving the result in dilute caustic soda. The raw material used is either cotton linters or wood pulp, which is boiled in caustic soda and then washed and compressed into sheets. After storage in a moist atmosphere, the sheets are steeped in caustic soda, which is then removed. The residue is shredded into crumbs, forming alkali cellulose. The white crumbs are kept for two or three days to allow a chemical reaction and then treated with carbon disulphide, turning orange to form cellulose xanthate. This is dissolved in a dilute solution of caustic soda, forming an orange viscous solution. Lustre may be controlled at this stage by adding pigment if a lustrous fibre is not required. After ripening and filtering the liquid is in a suitable state for spinning, which is done by forcing it through a spinneret, a small metal cap pierced by up to 3000 tiny holes. This extrusion of viscous liquid is a direct imitation of the way a silkworm spins its thread, hence the original term, artificial silk. The jets enter a bath containing a mixture of sulphuric acid and sulphates which convert the xanthate back to cellulose, which is insoluble, and the viscose filaments are formed.

CUPRAMMONIUM RAYON The basic process of manufacturing cuprammonium rayon is very similar to viscose rayon, except that the raw material, cotton linters, is dissolved in a solution of copper and ammonia. After passing through the spinneret the filaments partially harden in hot water, being stretched also during this process. After passing through an acid bath the filaments, which are very fine and strong, are wound, skeined, washed and dried.

ACETATE RAYON The other rayons are pure cellulose, but acetate rayon is made from cellulose acetate, a chemical derivative of cellulose. The cotton linters is treated with acetic acid, and, by a mixture of heat and chemical action, cellulose acetate flakes are formed. These are then dissolved in acetone and water, and extruded through the spinneret. Meeting a stream of warm air, which evaporates the acetone, the solution hardens into filaments after having been slightly stretched to increase their strength. This is called dry-spinning; it is a simpler method than that used for spinning the other rayons, where the spinning takes place after the material leaves the bath by one of three methods, all of which call for complicated machinery.

All the rayon filaments may be cut into appropriate staple lengths, and spun to requirements on existing machinery. These rayons are used for a very wide range of yarns, varying from fine silk-like filaments to coarse carpet yarns of varying strength, lustre and dyeing properties. Their advantages over the natural cellulose fibres are that they have a high lustre, which can be controlled as required; the supply, and therefore the price, is not subject to seasonal variations of weather or disease; they need no initial scouring, for there are no impurities; they are more uniform than natural fibres. Acetate responds to disperse dyestuffs, but the others may be dyed with cotton dyes.

ALGINATE RAYON This form of rayon is produced from the alginate acid extracted from seaweed. As it is soluble in soapy water it might seem to have limited use, but this property is useful in the weaving of fine fabrics as a carrier thread for strength, as a backing for lace, and as a scaffolding thread in the production of unusual woven effects. Alginate rayon is not inflammable, so it can also be used for theatre curtains.

Protein fibres Various fibres have been regenerated from proteins, which behave rather like wool. CASEIN, made from milk, is sold as Fibrolane, mainly for carpets and felts. A fibre made from groundnuts, called ARDIL, was produced, but its manufacture was suspended in 1959. A similar fate met VICARA, a maize based protein fibre, made in the USA, and another attempt with a soya-bean base was equally unsuccessful. In Germany, a fibre was produced from hides, but this, too, failed. All these have been attempts to make a fibre from commercial waste products, and no doubt further experiments will be successful, as in the modern world the necessity for re-cycling waste matter is becoming increasingly important.

Man-made fibres
Nylon The first truly man-made fibre was the polyamide, nylon, developed between 1928 and 1938 by W. H. Carothers in the research laboratories of Du Pont de Nemours, USA. The initial research was concerned with building up the different long-chain molecules which make rubbers and plastics, and it was discovered that if one of these was drawn out in a molten state, a yarn could result. When it was stretched to three or four times its length it became strong, lustrous and elastic, making an ideal hosiery yarn. By May 1940 the first nylon stockings were on sale in the USA.

The manufacture of nylon is similar to that of the rayons. The raw materials are coal or petroleum, air and water, which are chemically converted into a substance which becomes molten when heated. A ribbon of this substance falls on to a slowly moving wheel, cooled by water. A tough plastic material is formed, and this is broken into chips which are again heated and made molten in order to be extruded through the spinneret, hardening into a fibre on contact with air. The filaments are then stretched by passing through rollers moving at different speeds, becoming stronger and translucent in the process. If a coloured or less lustrous fibre is required pigments are added before extrusion. Nylon is thermo-plastic, which means that it can be permanently set by heating, which tends to melt it. Fabrics made from nylon may be permanently pleated because of this property, which was something new in the treatment of fibres. Because of its smooth nature, which is like a straight-sided tube, it does not absorb moisture well and therefore dries quickly, not an advantage when worn next the skin, but useful in many other ways. Because of its strength it is ideal for hosiery which was its first important use. Because it is soft, it can be blended with wool and cotton to give added strength, and because it can be spun into a very fine filament it is ideal for shirts and underwear. It is difficult to imagine now what life was like before nylon was discovered; darning socks and stockings was a major chore before the invention of this wonder fibre, not to mention ironing. Its combination of strength, lustre, lightness, crease-resistance, heat-setting ability and non-iron properties has led to the freeing of women from a great deal of domestic drudgery. Its use has permeated many areas of domestic use, including sheets, carpets, fur fabrics and outerwear as well as underwear.

Terylene A polyester fibre, again a derivative from petroleum, but this time combined with ethylene glycol, or antifreeze. Terylene was discovered by Dr J. T. Dickson and J. R. Whinfield, working for the Calico Printers Association in England in 1941, though the Second World War held up development until 1947, when it was developed and manufactured by I.C.I. It was also developed in the USA and from 1951 was known there as Dacron. Its construction and manufacture is similar to nylon, but because its molecules are very close together it is difficult for dyestuffs to penetrate. Special dyeing techniques are used which make use of its thermo-plastic property. Terylene has all the properties of nylon, and in addition it feels warmer, so that it is particularly suitable for blending with wool when it is crimped to resemble it, for suitings and carpet yarns.

Orlon, Acrilan and Courtelle These are all acrylic fibres and similar to each other in construction, initially developed from the American wartime synthetic rubber industry. The polymers which form the raw material are dissolved in solvents to make them viscous. When the solution is extruded through the spinneret the solvent evaporates in the air and the fibre solidifies. It is then stretched and treated in a similar way to the other synthetics. These fabrics are warm and soft as well as strong, and are used for a wide variety of yarns and clothing.

Polypropylene These are hardwearing, transparent fibres which are made in ribbon, sheet and monofilament form. They are used for carpets, car seat covers, sacking, and for ropes and cordage.

The advent of the synthetic fibres has revolutionised the textile industry. Because the raw materials are chemical, the product is not subject to the setbacks of variations in climate, pests and disease. The characteristics can be modified, so that a wide variety of materials may be produced by altering the formula, the processing, or the fibre length. There is, however, a danger which could alter the balance again: a shortage of synthetic textiles could follow a world shortage of petroleum, and this could result in the return to popularity of the natural fibres.

Glass fibre Fibres made of glass have been known since the 1890's and commercially produced with increasing success since the 1930's. Glass marbles are heated and drawn out into a filament which can be used for weaving decorative and fireproof fabrics. The fibre is strong, non-absorbent, fireproof and rotproof, and is used also in bulk form for insulation and soundproofing. It should be handled with care, as the tiny filaments can break off and irritate the skin.

2 Investigating materials

Yarns

Textile materials, as we have seen, have very individual characteristics and ways of behaving. Before these materials are used for any textile project it is useful to experiment with them to find out what these characteristics are in a practical way. Since it is unlikely that the raw fibres will be readily available, a selection of parcel strings, knitting wool or any other yarn should be collected. Weaver friends may be prepared to let you have waste ends of warp. The yarns will come in various weights, plies and, in the case of the strings, natural colours. The strings, too, may be knotted in ways which may suggest a design. The object of this exercise is to develop decorative forms from the natural behaviour of the material, without forcing it into shapes which are alien to it.

Presented with a miscellaneous collection of yarns (fig. 8), try to think yourself back into a childhood state in which you are looking at, and feeling, the yarns for the first time, using your eyes and fingers sensitively. Note whether the yarn is hard or soft; rough or smooth; lustrous or dull; elastic or inelastic; whether it assumes a shape easily, or whether it is too resilient. This is not as simple as it may seem, and demands concentration. The yarn will probably be plied, that is, several strands of spun yarn may be twisted together to make the yarn harder and stronger. A cabled yarn may have the plied yarns plied again, twisting in the opposite

8 A collection of various weights of yarn

9 When small lengths of sisal were separated they looked like flower heads, so the student drew in the stems with chalk

direction, to give even more hardness and strength. Try untwisting these plies first of all; the spun fibres may look rather different, being softer and taking the impress of the plying, and may tend at this stage to assume a simple pattern. Then separate the individual fibres, and you will find that surprising things begin to happen. The appearance of the fibres is often much softer, more lustrous, and altogether more delicate looking than the original yarn. Very often the fibres are reminiscent of other forms, such as flowers, figures, etc. and these may be developed in any way that suggests itself (fig. 9). It is important, however, not to have any particular 'picture' in mind beforehand, and any recognisable shapes that do develop should spring from the behaviour of the material itself rather than from a preconceived idea. Knots in the yarn may be an advantage, and can be used as a starting point to develop an idea. An open mind should be brought to these initial experiments, and it does not matter very much whether a shape develops or not, as the main importance lies in finding out about the yarns, how they are made, and how they behave. Fine emery paper makes a good background for these experiments, as its dark colour provides a contrast to the natural colours of the yarns and it will hold the fibres in position when they are pressed lightly into the surface. If you wish to keep the results of these experiments in a more permanent form they can be lightly attached to dark sugar paper with a transparent PVA adhesive. Just enough should be used to attach the yarn or fibre without overdoing it, or a series of shiny blobs will appear which will not be part of the intended result.

29

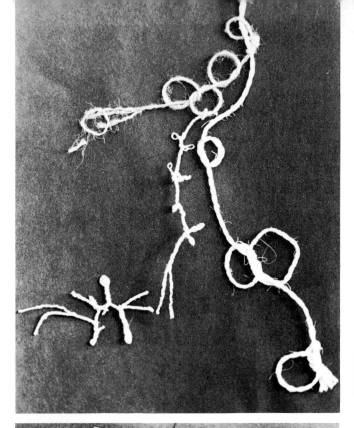

10 The beginnings of an idea. String has been looped, separated and distorted by pulling strands

11 This head of a girl evolved from a piece of sisal knotted and frayed

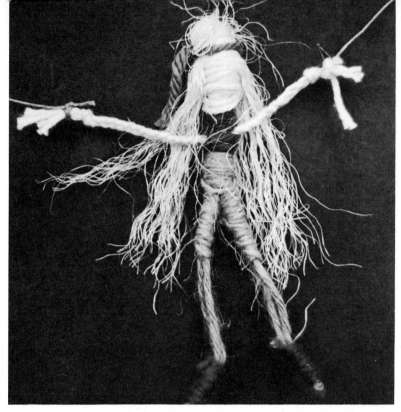

12 Bound jute made this figure, with cotton arms and sisal hair

By these means a knowledge of fibres will be acquired by the eye and the fingers, and will not be as easily forgotten as purely theoretic learning. Ideas may be generated which could be applied to embroidery, weaving, macramé and other textile exercises, and the knowledge of fibres is gained in a creative way.

Now consider the yarns themselves. See how they behave by bending, twisting, tying, plaiting (braiding) and knotting them in order to find out how best they can be used (fig. 10). The softer strings will knot easily to form lumps which will alter the linear character of the yarn by interrupting the continuity. By simple knotting, in regular or irregular sequence, patterns may evolve which could be used decoratively. This could be carried out as a group project on a large scale, using strings of varying characteristics which may also be dyed in different colours to enhance the effect. Certain yarns, like sisal, will tend to knot less readily and shapes in space will be made by the looping together of these yarns (fig. 11). The thicker the yarns the less easy it will be to hold the forms and the only way to secure them will be to bind them together with a thinner, softer piece of yarn. As soon as the idea of binding occurs, all sorts of more sophisticated shapes are possible (fig. 12). By combinations of binding, coiling and looping with strings of varying thickness and resilience, a great variety of three-dimensional forms becomes possible, and the knowledge of the fibres previously acquired can be brought into use.

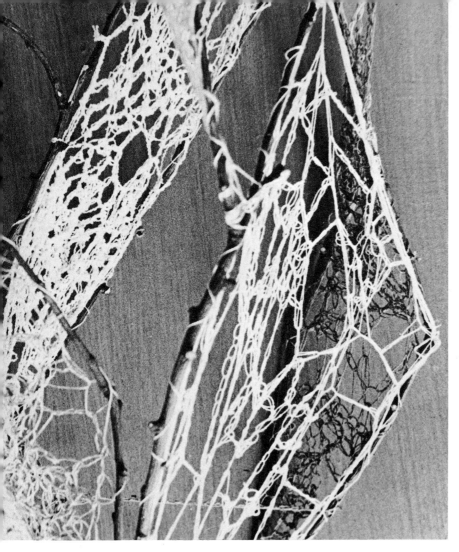

13 Detail from a crocheted construction based on a branched shrub. Crocheted freely in pale yellow and green linens and fancy cottons, the finished form shows an interesting relationship between the solid and open areas

The looping of yarns together may originally have led to the more formal processes of knitting and crochet, and the construction of garments. These techniques can be used in a freer way to create decorative forms (fig 13). Again a collection of yarns is necessary, in the widest variation of thickness, colour and texture. Start by casting on a few stitches with the usual size needles for the thickness of the yarn and, after knitting a few rows, alter the size of the needle, making it contrast violently with the yarn thickness. Experiment in this way, using fine yarn with enormous needles, and vice versa, observing the differences in the quality of the fabric. Cast off and stretch the work on to strawboard, pinning it out with straight pins, when you will find that it will very likely assume a different shape from the one envisaged when still on the needles. The pinning should be related to the natural stretch of the fabric, but it can be pinned out in different ways. The same exercise may be repeated with a crocheted fabric. Now experiment with casting on and off, still using contrasted yarns and increasing and decreasing in a random way; the effects of distortion will be even more strongly marked, and can result in a three-dimensional effect. If, in addition, stitches are picked up from the original shape and knitted or crocheted in different yarns, colours and tensions, the resulting forms, when stretched, can be very exciting. These first experiments should be carried out very freely and in a random manner, not necessarily counting stitches. The subsequent stretching is the final development of the form, whether in crochet or knitting, with loose, open structures on very large needles or hooks juxtaposed with close textures.

After experiment comes control, and exercises can now follow with a greater knowledge of what is possible. There are no set rules for this, but you should make your own rule and keep to it. For instance, you may decide that you are going to work in units of five, which means that you could start with five, ten, or fifteen stitches, and every five rows cast on five at each side, varying the yarn and needles at each change. You could then decide to increase at every fifth thread for five rows, and so on. This obviously has the beginnings of some fan-like shape, but it all depends on the contrast of yarns and needles, and what sort of curve the stretched shape will assume as a result. The stiffer and thicker the yarn the more the form will keep its own shape, and the larger the shape will be, until sharpened broom handles become the only feasible form of knitting needle! The final shapes must be stiffened with dilute PVA adhesive, as described in detail on page 40, so that the form is held without altering the appearance of the fabric.

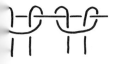

Macramé heading

Macramé is the Arabic name for the technique of knotting decorative forms currently having its third revival in this country; the second was in Victorian times, and it first became popular a century earlier. The yarns used must be smooth, firm, and fairly tightly twisted, in order to give clarity to the pattern and to help hold the shape. A heading thread, tightly stretched, is required for the first experiments. This can be tied to clamps on a table, or stretched on a chairback. Doubled threads are looped on to this heading in pairs (fig. 14), with the ends of the threads drawn through the loop. Each pair of threads makes the four single threads of the working unit. The two outside threads are the working ones, the two centre threads forming the cord, which does not move and should be kept taut. Sinnets can be made from these four threads by tying what is virtually a reef knot round the cords (fig. 15), making sure that the centre cord is always caught

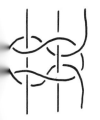

Macramé: sinnet or ɪare knot

between the knot. The knot is tied in two halves; if the first half is repeated the sinnet will spiral one way, if only the second half of the knot is used it will spiral the other way. If both halves are tied and repeated the result will be a flat braid. One set of threads may be split and joined to the next set, and this splitting and joining is the basis of designing in macramé. Belts and small hangings could be attempted in sinnet knots alone, but there is another basic knot used in macramé – the half-hitch – which produces a different sort of patterning. A simple half-hitch makes a single loop round a taut thread (fig. 16). The usual form of this knot, however, is the double half-hitch used in cording. It is worked over a foundation cord and can be worked in various directions as dictated by the requirements of the design. Each thread attached to the foundation cord is given a half-hitch twice round it, whether the foundation cord is horizontal, vertical or diagonal. The first row is usually composed of horizontal double half-hitches (fig. 17), which spaces out the loops, and the threads must be pulled very tight in order to keep the shape. The easiest way of starting macramé is to loop threads round the centre bar of a buckle until it is comfortably filled, and to work with these two simple knots, allowing the pattern to evolve as the work progresses, using a jute twine, or loom cord, which will be stiff enough to hold the shape. With the experience gained a small hanging could be attempted, looping the initial number of threads round a dowel rod. It is difficult to estimate the length of yarn required for macramé projects, as the working threads and the foundation threads can be interchanged if the pattern dictates it. As a rough guide, about four and a half times the finished length would be about right for each thread, with an extra allowance for any fringing. The yarns can, in any case, be joined by splicing them together, as in knitting or crochet work, or finer yarns can be used double for a short distance. Each length of yarn should be rolled up into a small bundle for easy working, or rolled round a piece of card.

Collages may be made from yarn. Once again, consider the character of the yarns you intend to use – whether it is soft and pliable, or hard and springy, tightly plied or loosely spun, hairy or smooth – because all these characteristics will affect the final design. The yarn is glued on to fairly thick cardboard with PVA adhesive. For the first attempt choose white, slightly stiff string of medium weight. Spread a little of the adhesive on the card and coil the string, pressing it down firmly either with the fingers or with a small pad of clean cloth until it is held in position. Do not use too much adhesive or it will come through to the surface. If it does, wipe it off at once before it dries, or transparent patches will show over the string. Use the string as continuously as possible and follow the shapes it will tend to make naturally, gradually covering the surface of the card and spreading the adhesive over small areas as the work proceeds. The shadows cast by the string will form part of the pattern, and different thicknesses of string could be used to enhance this effect. The linear nature of the string will form flowing patterns reminiscent of water and wood grain.

16 Macramé: half hitch

17 Macramé: double half hitch

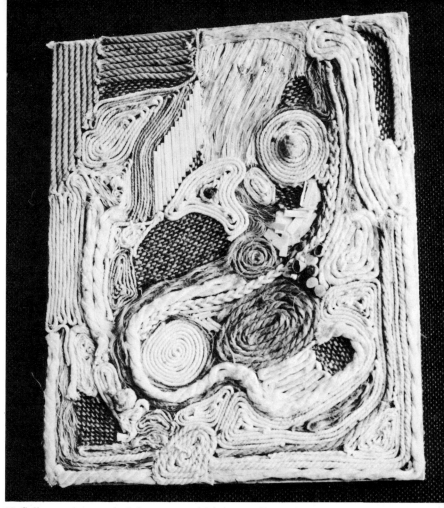

18 Collage, using matchsticks, paper and fabric as well as strings

Further experiments can follow with different weights of string in different natural shades, and then with different yarns and colours; when larger pieces are attempted, sketch out roughly the areas of pattern to be filled. If you have a number of yarns you wish to use, but not in the colours you require, one solution could be to spray the piece with gold or silver paint after it is completed, which gives it a homogeneity it would not otherwise have. The materials used will always dominate this type of design, so the result should not be forced but kept within the character of the medium. Do not attempt too large an area at once, or the adhesive will stick to your hands and clothing or dry before the area is finished. With a little experience the pattern can be planned, at least in outline, and neat ways of working will evolve which will minimise the annoyance of loose yarns coming into contact with the adhesive when not intended. These experiments with yarns are very satisfying for beginners of all ages, as the scale of the operation makes for quick results (fig. 18).

19 Stitched mathematical shape

A more organised way of using finer threads is by stitching them into card to make mathematically based patterns. Simple, basic shapes are drawn on the card, and holes are pricked at carefully measured intervals round the shape. Lines are then sewn across the shape, between the holes, with each end of the lines moving along one hole in opposite directions (fig. 19). The movement of the lines makes mathematical curves, and may be built up to form interlinking patterns. If suitable colour combinations are used for the yarns the resulting interchange of colour and pattern can be very subtle. This exercise is also a very suitable one for school use. A number of experiments should be made, using different forms of mathematical shapes such as squares, rectangles, triangles, circles, angles, etc., and from these experiments a more three-dimensional form of the same patterns may be constructed on nails driven into a suitable background.

Fabric
Just as string is an easily obtainable material to use for textile investigation, so loosely woven, coarse fabric is a suitable material for the creative investigation of cloth. Coarse jute sacking may be available from commercial organisations and shops as waste material, especially if it is to be used for educational purposes; onion, carrot and potato bags may usually be begged from a friendly greengrocer; very loose jute scrim, sometimes used as packaging round the roots of plants, is excellent if it is washed before it has rotted away.

Woven fabric is composed of interlaced threads crossing one another at an angle of ninety degrees. It is fairly easy to distort the weave of the chosen material by pulling out threads in one or both directions. The holes and spaces formed may then be further distorted by pulling. Start with a small piece of fabric, about 30 cm (12 ins) square, and pull out a few threads. This may suggest other ways of removing them so as to form a pattern of spaces. This pattern can then be embellished by re-using the pulled threads, re-weaving, knotting and fringing them until the surface of the material has been completely altered. Try pulling a few threads without removing them; this will alter the surface in a different way, so that the cloth puckers and becomes three-dimensional. At this stage no needles will be used, as the fingers will be doing the work. Poke holes into the fabric (fig. 20), and a different kind of distortion will take place, the holes being surrounded by threads which are packed together to form the shape of the hole. By this time, the haphazard pulling may begin to assume forms, and

20 A drama student's interpretation of pulled holes. Red and green carrot bags were used for these simple masks of tragedy and comedy

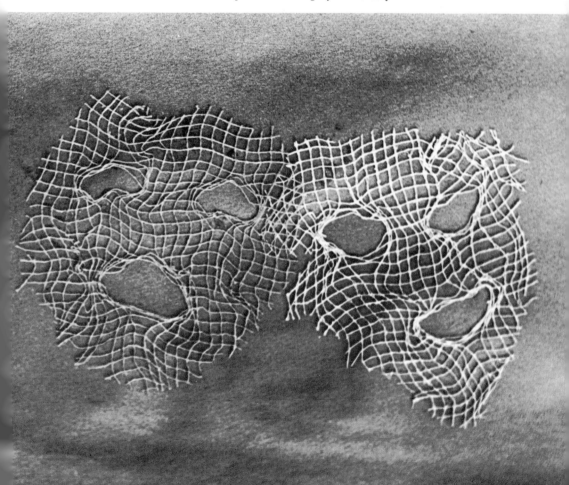

further decoration of the surface will be needed. Coarse needles may then be used (fig. 21) and, in addition to any pulled threads, other suitable threads such as the strings used for the previous exercise may be introduced (fig. 21). If this is being carried out with a class of beginners be careful not to introduce too great a variety of other yarns at this stage, for the essence of the exercise is experimentation with the material itself and the imaginative use of what is there. In addition, restriction of the materials to fibres which harmonise is important, especially if woven polypropylene sacking is used. This material slides apart easily, but does not tend to hold a shape so well as jute, so the added threads may have to be functional as well as decorative.

With the use of needles, the beginnings of embroidery appear. Beginners of all ages should be encouraged to experiment in a very free way with stitches, again using pulled threads from the material or contrasting strings, and using the needle to make random stitches in any direction. No attempt at formal stitchery should be made yet but shapes may be suggested and a 'picture' developed (fig. 22). By now the threads themselves will have become interesting, and this interest can be developed through the behaviour of the thread, in a similar way to the ideas for yarn collage, as a start to true embroidery. Starting with a thick, fairly flexible thread, hold it above the fabric and let the end gently settle down on to the surface. This will make a simple thread pattern. By adding other threads in varied weights, colours and textures, and using both plain and fancy yarns, more complex patterns will emerge, and the threads may be controlled to produce patterns at will. At this stage stitching will not be necessary as the threads can be lightly fixed to the surface with PVA adhesive. The waste warp left over from weaving, and odd pieces of yarn from other

21 Coarse, stained sacking which has been wrapped round the roots of a plant suggested a two-tone face which has been further embellished with contrasting string and sisal

22 The student started by pulling out regular sequences of threads, which did not suggest anything. Random stitching with string evolved into this bull-like shape, with a piece of twisted jute fibre, lightly knotted and bound, to form the rider

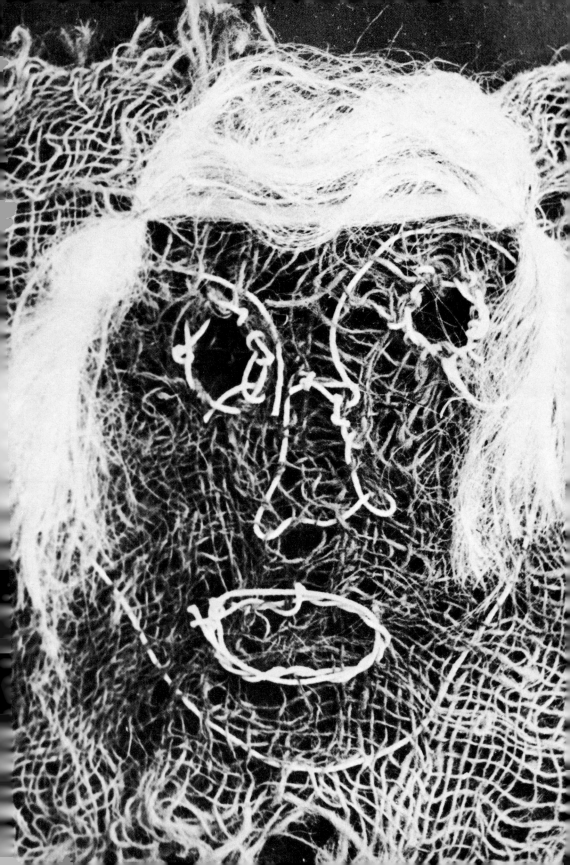

activities, should always be saved for these experimental efforts, while the experiments themselves should be kept as a form of notebook for future ideas. In addition, yarns can be wound round cards and tubes, forming crossing patterns and texture which can spark off ideas for embroidery. After a few attempts a design may emerge which is worth preserving in a more permanent form. To do this use the simple couching stitch, which consists of a finer thread sewn over the pattern thread to hold it down firmly to the background (fig. 23). As skill progresses and more confidence is gained, other embroidery stitches may be introduced as a way of filling in space and creating texture, using the stitchery to create an overall impression of colour, solidity, space and shape rather than as an end in itself. Formal stitches may be used in a very free way by varying the size of the stitches, changing their direction and using different thicknesses of thread. These experiments with yarn and stitchery can go hand-in-hand until a satisfactory design is achieved.

23 Couching a thread

When using coarse materials you will find that the thread constantly slips through the eye of the needle. Anchor it by pulling out a reasonable length of 'tail' and threading the needle back through the twist of the main part of the thread (fig. 24). When pulled tight, the tail is caught through the length of the thread and held by the tension of the stitching.

All forms of these creative uses of yarns and fabrics may be made more permanent by the use of PVA adhesive for stiffening. A tablespoon of adhesive to a pint of water, well mixed, will stiffen the fabric without altering its character. Flat fabrics may be placed on a sheet of polythene and well soaked with the PVA solution, then blotted with a clean piece of cotton cloth or a paper towel to remove the surface moisture, and peeled off the polythene when dry. Three-dimensional forms must be carefully dampened rather than soaked, or the solution will run, and then left to dry. Fabric may also be stiffened in this way for first attempts at embroidery so that the material is easier to handle.

24 Catching the tail of embroidery thread

Having discovered the characteristics of certain types of thread and fabric, the knowledge could be used to create a fabric collage. A collage is an assemblage of materials glued on to a background to make a design. It may be pictorial or non-representational, and is a way of drawing with scissors and assembling the shapes to make the design. Before you begin, make a collection of fabrics, yarns, beads, buttons, sequins, lace etc.

As you have been working with fairly neutral tones of fabric and thread the projects could be related by looking at objects which are themselves made up of the same neutral tones. Examine buildings, stones, landscapes, newspaper photographs, patterns on wood grain and water, shells, birds, tree bark, and cut out the shapes found in any of these. Arrange the pieces on a backing. Experiments may be glued straight on to cardboard, but for more finished pieces of work a fabric background is desirable. When a

25 Collage from paper, fabric, braid and crayon made by a six-year-old

satisfactory arrangement of the shapes has been reached, decide what further additions are needed in the form of thread etc. These will be necessary to reinforce the line of the design and to provide textural interest, and have to be carefully considered. The gluing is carried out with PVA adhesive, using only enough to make the fabric adhere or it will soak through and mark the surface. The design possibilities may be extended not only by using threads, buttons etc., but also by the distortion of fabric in the ways I have already described. (A very effective collage I particularly remember from a students' exhibition had small folds of natural hessian (burlap) glued to resemble hills in a landscape, with the folds reinforced by fine lines of thread.) From these simple beginnings more complicated work should evolve when fabrics of different colours, textures and patterns are used, bringing into play the knowledge of fibres and fabrics acquired earlier.

All the exercises with fabric and thread may be used as a group project, each member of the group being responsible for a detail of the design. Coarse hessian (burlap) and jute scrim may be purchased by the yard, and compositions on a large scale are possible if the fabric is joined. If old sacks are used they could be joined together, the stitching forming part of the design.

Finished collages require mounting (matting). An allowance of about 5 cm (2 ins) should be left round the design so that the backing fabric can be folded over a piece of stiff cardboard. Opposite edges should be stitched together with long stitches across the back, pulling the collage tightly to stretch it and making sure that the grain of the backing material lies evenly (fig. 26). Then treat the other two edges in the same way, and the collage is ready to be framed. If desired, it can be glued to a larger mount (mat) before framing.

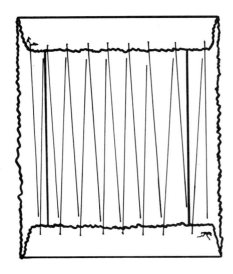

26 Stitching the collage over the back of the cardboard

3 Spinning

Most textile fibres can be spun into a yarn, with varying degrees of success, but wool is the easiest fibre to use because of its construction. It is possible to buy ready-sorted wool called matchings, and there are also wool staplers from whom whole fleeces may be obtained. Fleece collected from hedgerows is suitable too.

There are differences of opinion about the initial washing, or scouring, of wool. If the spun yarn is to be used in its natural colour I prefer to spin it in its own grease, for not only does this enable the fleece to be spun easily, but it also makes the hands very soft and white in the process. For first attempts a medium staple such as a Welsh Mountain fleece is preferable. First of all, the obvious impurities, such as dirt from the tail end, thorns, burrs, thistles etc., have to be removed. The fleece must then be sorted into qualities, the best being found on the flanks, the worst on the extremities and places like the neck where it gets rubbed. The fleece varies in length and fineness on various parts of the body, and divides fairly obviously into separate locks. Take one of these in the left hand and, employing a slightly downward movement to take advantage of the overlapping scale structure of the fibre, draw each fibre sideways between the thumb and the bent forefinger of the right hand, separating it from the rest. The aim is to spread out the fibres, let the air in and the dirt out, so as you separate let the dirt fall to the ground. The resulting airy mass should not be crushed up in the hand but allowed to fall away, when it will usually cling lightly together without actually falling to the ground. This process is called teasing. When a small pile has accumulated, take this lightly between the fingers and draw it out gently, placing the fibres together again. Do this several times until the fibres are all lying more or less parallel. It is most important to handle the fibres lightly at this stage, otherwise they will pack down solidly together again.

If carders are not available it is possible to spin straight from the teased fleece, especially if the fleece itself is of good quality; the fleece should be spread out slightly, still keeping the fibres parallel, and lightly rolled up to form a hollow cylinder. It is, however, desirable to straighten the fibres further, and this is achieved by carding.

Wool cards are rectangular pieces of wood covered with leather through which pairs of bent steel wires protrude, and each card has a handle attached to the side. The wool is drawn between the two cards through the wire teeth. Place the cards back to back, with the handles projecting on opposite sides so that the upper one with its handle to the left is resting on the lower one with its handle to the right. Spread small pieces of teased fleece lightly on the surface of the left-hand, upper card. Grasp the handles, with both thumbs underneath, and without changing the position of the hands turn the upper card over and lightly stroke it with the right-hand one, two or three times, giving it a slight rocking upward movement. Repeat this several times until the fleece is evenly spread over the card. Then, still keeping the same grip on the handles, bring the fronts of the cards together and draw the right-hand card through the left-hand one with a steady upward movement, so that the fleece is transferred to the right-hand card (fig. 27a); the small fringe of fleece which hangs from the bottom of the card assists this process by catching on to the other card. Repeat this movement in reverse, still keeping the same grip as before, and continue transferring the fleece from one card to the other until the fibres are even and parallel. After the last transfer, keep the fronts of the cards together and brush one card sharply downwards to remove the fleece. If it still tends to stick it can be removed by hand, as it should be only lightly adhering to the wires. It is important to make all these movements as lightly as possible and to keep the fleece on the surface of the card. If the carding produces too much noise, or it becomes so difficult that the cards drag, then there is either too much fleece or you are digging the fleece too far into the card.

Good cards have slightly curved backs to facilitate the next stage. Lay the fleece on the back of one of the cards and, using the small fringe that protruded each time the fleece was carded, start rolling up the fleece with the cards back to back, again using very light movements, until you have a hollow cylinder with the fibres lying round it in a horizontal direction (fig. 27b). This is called a rolag (a Swedish word meaning roll), and is the basis of a woollen yarn, as opposed to a worsted yarn.

A worsted yarn is made from one of the longwool fleeces, which are lustrous and strong. The fleece is teased in the same way, but instead of being carded it is held by a lock and drawn through the teeth of a comb. A fairly good improvisation may be made from a nylon hair-styling brush with strong smooth points. The handle is clamped to a table, and the lock is held by one end and drawn through the teeth until the short fibres are removed. It is then turned round and held by the other end and the process is repeated. The straight parallel fibres which remain are called tops, and the short ends, or noils, are used for woollen yarns.

Owing to its structure, which in a handspun yarn takes the same form as the rolag, a woollen yarn is warm because air is trapped inside it, and also because the fibres protrude from it at right angles to the length of the yarn. The way a woollen yarn is spun is designed to keep the structure of the rolag, and a hand spindle produces a high quality, rounded yarn, full of 'bounce'.

A hand spindle may be bought, made, or easily improvised; it is in essence a stick pushed through a weight called a whorl. My

27b The rolag rolled on the carved back of the card

27a Carding: the fleece is spread out and drawn between the cards

28 Carding; the fleece is being drawn through the cards

29 Children spinning on spindles improvised from potatoes; a holiday activity at Warrington Museum

favourite improvisation, and one which is well balanced and the correct weight, is a 30-cm (12-in) wooden meat skewer pushed through half a medium-size potato (fig. 29). With experience you will be able to judge the exact weight which will allow the yarn to spin easily but not be so heavy as to break it, especially when the spindle is full. The whorl may be solid and cone shaped, or flat, or various shapes in between. The pointed stick (which could be a discarded knitting needle) should fit tightly into the central hole, wedged in with a piece of yarn if necessary.

A length of spun woollen yarn is needed to start the process. Make a slip loop in the end of it, and slip it over the top of the spindle until it rests on the whorl. Tighten the loop and pass the yarn under the whorl and up the other side, winding it once round the pointed end of the spindle on the way. Continue the yarn up to the top of the spindle, and secure it with a half-hitch (fig. 30). You will now need several more hands than you have, and it is better to work with another person until you can control your hand movements. Set the spindle spinning, while holding the yarn in your left hand. Hold the rolag between the thumb and first finger of the same hand, with most of it hanging over the back of the hand

30 Spindle with t yarn tied and looped a half hitch

46

31 Four hands are better than two at first, but even a six-year-old can quickly learn to spin. Note the way the rolag rests over the hand so that it does not entangle in the spinning

(fig. 31), so that it does not catch in the spun yarn. You will feel the yarn tighten against your fingers as it becomes overspun, and the end of the fleece may then be caught round it and incorporated; the overlapping structure of the fibre helps it to catch on to the yarn. Continue spinning the spindle, holding the yarn about one inch away from the rolag until the spin tightens against the fingers again. Release your hold on the rolag and move your thumb and finger back along it. Grasp it again, drawing it out as you do so. The spin already in the inch of yarn will travel up the fleece and start to make the new yarn. You will probably find that it is thick, and that there will be a little resistance as you try to draw it out. Release more of the rolag, while still drawing it out, remembering to open the fingers and close them again rather than dragging them up the rolag, and the yarn will become thinner. The characteristic form of the rolag will then be preserved in the yarn. It will be better initially if one person draws the fibre, and the other spins the spindle.

Repeat the process until the spun yarn becomes too long to manage, and then, keeping it at tension, wind it up in a figure-of-eight 'butterfly' on the left hand, between the thumb and little finger. Release the half-hitch which is supporting the yarn, undo the turn at the bottom of the spindle, and wind the yarn on to the spindle above the whorl, still keeping it at tension and winding it near the whorl rather than along the length of the spindle. The spun yarn is then secured to the top of the spindle in the same way as before, and the process is repeated until the spindle is full of yarn or becomes too heavy. You will find that the weight of the spindle affects the speed of spinning, and that too much weight will tend to break the yarn. The fineness of the spun yarn will depend on the fineness of the fibre.

A worsted yarn differs from woollen yarn as its requirements and uses differ. It is used where strength and smoothness are more important than warmth (for example, men's fine suitings) so the yarn must be fine and smooth rather than hairy. It should therefore be spun from a lustrous longwool fibre. Take the lock in the left hand and spin the yarn on the spindle with the right hand, while drawing out a group of fibres between the fingers of the left hand so that they form a triangular shape as they are incorporated into the yarn (fig. 32). The movement is much more confined than in woollen spinning. Go on doing this until the yarn becomes long enough to wind up, and proceed as before. Even if the same fibre is used for both processes the difference in the two types of yarn produced is quite striking.

Spun yarn has to be skeined for scouring and dyeing. It can be wound on a skeiner, or on the back of a chair, or in the traditional way on outstretched hands. When the skein is complete, knot the two ends together. Secure these two ends loosely through the skein in a figure-of-eight, with a piece of cotton yarn knotted in with them, leaving a long end hanging, and make three more figure-of-eight ties (fig. 33). Lay the skein in warm soapy water for a time until some of the dirt comes out. (Soap is better than detergent which may remove too much grease, making the wool harsh.) Repeat with fresh water until the yarn is clean, and then rinse in warm water. At no stage should the skein be rubbed or agitated violently, or the wool will felt. Wring it gently and hang it up to dry, preferably in an airy place. The yarn will be stretched by its own weight, emerging with a natural curl. A straighter yarn can be obtained by hanging a weight on the skein. This process sets the yarn, and it is then ready for weaving; if it is to be dyed first, it is essential that the ties are not in the least tight, or the dye will not be able to penetrate.

32 Spinning a wors ed yarn: the fleece drawn between th fingers to form a tr angle

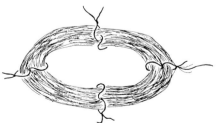

33 The skeined ya loosely tied with f ure-of-eight ties

4 Weaving

First experiments

A frequent objection to weaving as a craft, especially in schools, is that it is too complicated, too time-consuming, too expensive and takes up too much room. A loom is only a device across which warp threads are stretched so that weft threads can be woven across them, and there are many ways of making a simple structure for this purpose. A simple loom does not limit creative possibilities, and in some ways the process is more flexible than on a more complex mechanism. If we look at the work produced by so-called primitive people we find a very high level of artistic achievement, in spite of the fact that it may have been woven on what is virtually a collection of old sticks. More complex looms are merely extensions of these devices, the mechanism having been invented to speed up the weaving and produce longer lengths of cloth more easily and quickly.

Why then do we wish to weave by hand? Apart from the personal satisfaction of creation, a piece of work may be hand-woven in a way that is not possible with a commercial process. More expensive yarns may be used than is economic in industry, giving a better quality piece; yarns may be dyed to special requirements or specially spun; a more complex sequence of yarns and colours may be used than is possible on an industrial loom; surface decorations, such as knotting, binding etc., used perhaps in a random manner, can be incorporated. This means that the completed piece of work can be a genuine expression of individuality, not necessarily repeatable.

Pieces of ordinary cardboard, cut from box lids, cartons, etc. can be used for your first efforts, with oddments of weaving yarns, string, knitting wool etc. Start accumulating pieces of yarn well in advance of the project; if you are working with a group you can ask members of the group to bring in their own collection of yarns. Think in terms of a 'picture', not as an exact representation, but as an interpretation in yarns. A collection of reproductions of paintings, either in the form of postcards or cuttings from magazines, is helpful in providing ideas for colour and shape. These should be carefully chosen for their colour mixtures and textural interest, and may be made more abstract by cutting them into pieces so that there is less temptation to copy recognisable objects in a pictorial way; this should be an exercise in mixing yarns rather than an attempt at exact reproduction. The idea is to imitate the colours and shapes found in the reproduction, introducing the effect of the texture produced by paint in the original by whatever weaving technique seems to be appropriate. Look closely at the picture you are going to work from and decide whether the yarns you have are exactly right, or whether there is a

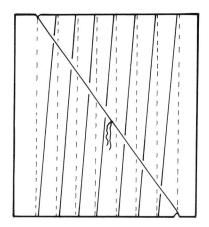

mixture of colours in the reproduced paint. Yarns may be mixed in the same way, using two or three or more at a time, and you will find you can vary the number of shades with only a limited number of yarns by varying the proportions of each colour. A good exercise in this connection is to try to grade yarns from one range of colours to another, using three shades of yarn at a time and dropping one and adding another after a few rows of weaving, so that the colour gradually changes.

Having carefully chosen your yarns for the warp, wrap them round the card, spacing them evenly or unevenly and remembering that wide or close spacing will produce different texture in the weaving. The spacing will depend on the thickness of the yarns and how much you want them to appear in the finished design. The card can have a small slit cut at the beginning and end of the warp to hold the threads in place while they are being joined across the back of the card (fig. 34), but it is not necessary to notch the edges of the card all the way along. The warp must be chosen with care because it will make its contribution to the design, sometimes showing and sometimes hidden by the weft.

35 A textured weav

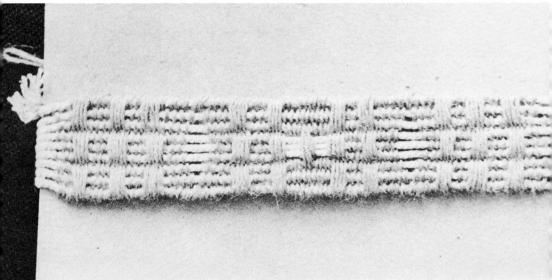

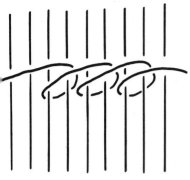

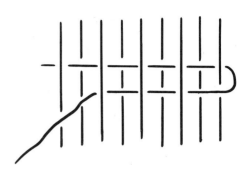

6 Soumak weave

37 The end of the thread carried back over the warp

A curved bodkin is used to carry the weft yarn over and under the warp in a simple darning process, which produces a weave. The texture of the paint in your picture can be reproduced in several ways. You may find that you have textured yarns, or you can make your own by knotting the yarn in various ways, or even by using torn-up strips of fabric. Another way is to take the weft over or under several warp threads at once, for several rows, so that the warp is covered in some places and exposed in others (fig. 35). Warp yarns can be bound together by wrapping the weft round them, or the weft can be passed over several warp threads and then back again under a smaller number (fig. 36). This is called Soumak and can be worked in single rows or in blocks with a row of regular weaving in between. The weft can also be looped and knotted round the warp. Colours need not be exactly the same as in the reproduction; the object is to learn how to mix yarns rather than using them as they come, though with a greater range of yarns a more exact reproduction would be possible and this is, in fact, how some tapestry weavers weave from a cartoon. The shapes need not be exact either, and you will find that ways of weaving tapestry will evolve naturally, and can be built upon later. As the need to make shapes arises, you will realise that the yarn need not be taken right across the warp but can be turned back at any point dictated by the design.

This is to be a decorative piece of work, and ends must not be left hanging on the surface or at the sides unless they are part of the design. On the first row, the loose end of yarn left after weaving must be tucked back into the same warp threads (fig. 37), and this tidying-up process must be repeated each time a colour is changed. The finished piece is cut at the back of the card and the warp ends are knotted together in pairs with an overhand knot (fig. 38); the piece is then usually suitable for window-mounting (matting) between sheets of cardboard (fig. 39). An adventurous use of yarns and textures on these first pieces of weaving can lead to more finished work later on.

38 Overhand knot

39 A piece of wea
ing mounted on whi
cardboard sandwiche
between layers
black paper. Note ho
the shapes and te
tures of the paintin
reproduced below a
carried out in t
yarns and weave

40 Weaving based
the shape of a la
twig, which adds
own texture. The sh
is further emphasi
by the curving si
yarn

Another way of weaving shapes on larger pieces of cardboard is to wind a fine thread at half-inch intervals round the card, knotting it at the back as before and using a neutral colour as this time the warp is not intended to play a major part in the design. By lifting alternate threads, a large twig with a curved or branching shape can be inserted between the threads and used to define woven forms, taking the weft yarn backwards and forwards across the warp within, or curved round, the shapes formed by the twig (fig. 40). This exercise is concerned with the selection of suitable yarns for a specific purpose, the relation of decorative weft patterns and, again, the beginnings of tapestry techniques, this time with more emphasis on conforming to a shape. When the warp threads are cut at the back they should be tied together in pairs with an overhand knot. The threads at one end can be knotted on to a straight stick with a split loop (fig. 41) and then cut short and concealed behind the work. The work can then be hung up by the stick, with the knotted threads at the other end left to form a fringe.

41 Split loop and ti

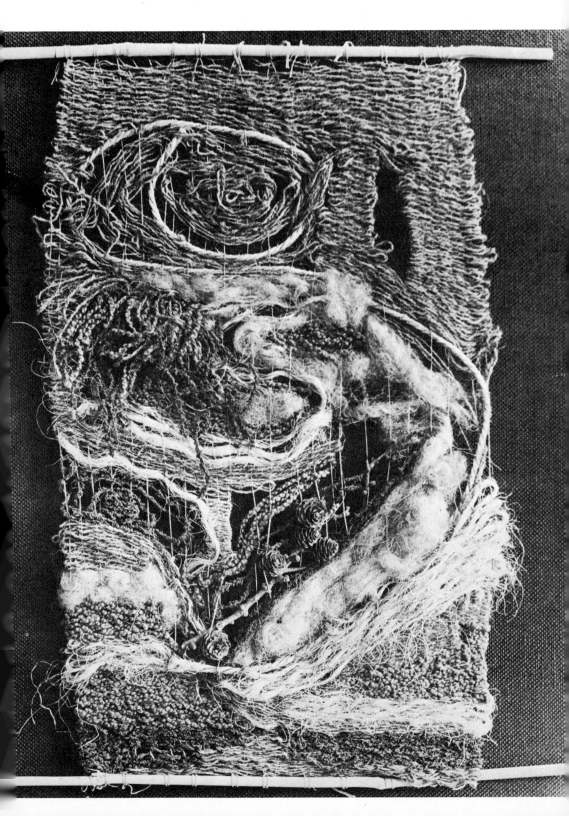

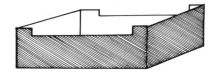

Simple looms and frames

While experimenting with flat cardboard, you will find that the tension of the wound warp will bend the card into a bow shape, which will make weaving easier. Further experiments may be made with boxes and box lids; deeper boxes could have the sides cut away to make more room for weaving (fig. 42), with the warp wound round the ends of the box in exactly the same way as on the cardboard. These boxes are much more like a conventional loom, and at this stage we can consider making a simple loom or frame. There are several ways of doing this, and the easiest is to use a wooden tomato box with corner 'feet' which may be obtained for a few pence, or even free, from your local greengrocer. Drive a nail into each corner of the box (using fairly thin nails, as the wood tends to split easily) and bend the nail outwards slightly. A piece of dowel rod or garden cane can then be placed behind each pair of nails (fig. 43) and held in place by tying the two rods together with

42 A box with the side cut away to allow the shuttle to pass more easily

43 A tomato-box loom with nails. The very open weave uses the character of the sisal; some of the loops were later filled, the other left open

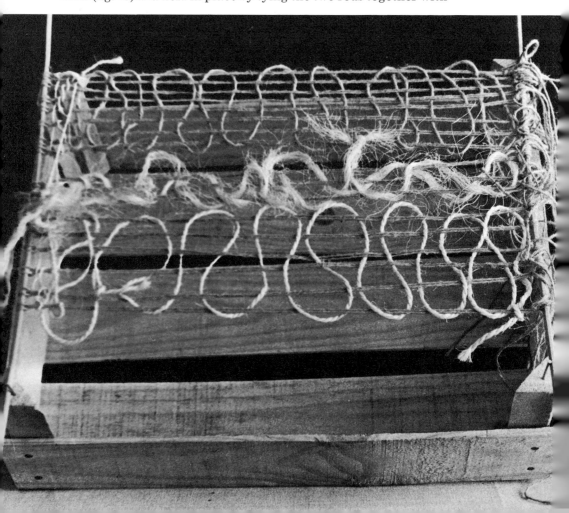

the split loop and knot shown in fig. 41. Instead of nails you could use large cup hooks, which hold the rods more easily. If the box is sandpapered before use it makes an excellent frame loom, as the projecting corners raise the warp above the level of the sides, making a space for the shuttle to pass across it. Another advantage is that yarns, shuttles, etc. may be kept in the box. The warp is tied in pairs between the rods, using the same knots as before and leaving extra length for a fringe if required. The tension must be neither too tight nor too loose but somewhere between the two extremes, keeping it even throughout; the weft yarns take up space as weaving progresses and tighten the warp, while a warp that is too loose will make the weft difficult to beat together closely. One rod can be left in when the weaving is finished, to be used as a hanger, in which case it must be carefully chosen to form part of the design. It is not possible to weave for the whole length of the warp, as the tension becomes too tight, and allowance must be made for this when designing the weaving. The colour and texture of the warp yarns should be carefully considered and the threads may be evenly spaced all the way across or arranged in groups, some close, others far apart. When tied, the warp is ready for weaving.

Weaving shuttles can be made from pieces of shaped wood (fig. 44) or even from strong cardboard, or may be purchased. My favourite small shuttle is a vulcanite one designed for netting, with a pointed end (fig. 45). This form of shuttle slides easily through the warp and is less liable to catch in it. The shuttle may be darned through the warp threads, as with the bodkin in card-weaving; or sheds (the spaces between alternate rows of warp through which the shuttle will pass) can be formed with two sticks darned in and out of alternate threads, leaving one permanently in and moving it to the other end of the weaving while the other is used. An even quicker method is to attach loops to the warp threads which the first stick passes over, so that they can be pulled up and the second stick becomes unnecessary (fig. 46).

Another type of frame loom can be constructed from four battens, approximately 2×5 cm ($\frac{3}{4} \times 2$ ins), one pair about 35 cm (14

44 Stick shuttle

45 Netting shuttle

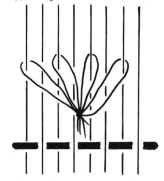

46 Loops attached to alternate warp threads

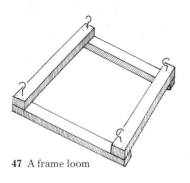

47 A frame loom

48 The warp can be ex
tended round the loom
Sticks A and C are in
serted in the cup hook
and a third stick, B, i
tied to A; when the
warp is moved round
the fourth stick, D,
placed in the empty
hooks

ins) long and the other 40 cm (16 ins). Screw the two shorter pieces on to the longer pieces to form the frame, with three screws at each corner for strength, and then screw cup hooks into the corners to hold the rods (fig. 47). This type of frame is flatter than the box frame, can be made in any size and, as an additional advantage, the warp can be extended round the frame by adding two extra rods as shown in fig. 48, allowing it to be moved round as weaving progresses. The wood should be stout enough to withstand the tension of the warp as it is tightened by weaving – the weak point in the otherwise excellent tomato-box frame is that it may split under tension. This frame may be used for various types of weaving from first experiments to small items like table mats, as well as, on a larger scale, for rugs and hangings. The same type of loom may be improvised from strong boxes or drawers, strengthening the corners where necessary.

Primitive looms

Other simple forms of loom can be constructed, based on the weaving methods of primitive societies. The simplest of these is the bow loom, made up of one stick and the warp threads. Choose a stick which is fairly flexible, bend it to form a bow shape, and tie the ends together with a piece of string so that the string is held taut by the tension of the bow. Then cut warp threads the same length as the string, and knot the ends together, keeping the tension even; the threads can be cut individually and laid on a table, or wound round a chairback or other convenient object of the right size and cut all together. Tie the warp to the stick with strong yarn passed through the knotted ends, and then cut the original piece of string so that the spring in the bowed stick will hold the warp at the required tension (fig. 49). You will not need a great number of threads for this type of weaving; it is mainly used for short braids, hairbands, belts, etc., and it is better at this stage to use thicker yarns and fewer threads so that they can more easily be kept in the correct order. As a refinement, to space the warp evenly, the threads could be passed through holes in a piece of card (fig. 50) or over the teeth of a comb; otherwise the weaving can be controlled by the fingers. The braids may be woven as an ordinary weave, or the warp may be closed together by pulling the weft in tightly, keeping the edges very even, so that it does not show and all the pattern is in the warp. Patterns of stripes or small squares

49 A bow loom ma
from a branch, wi
the warp attached
loops of yarn

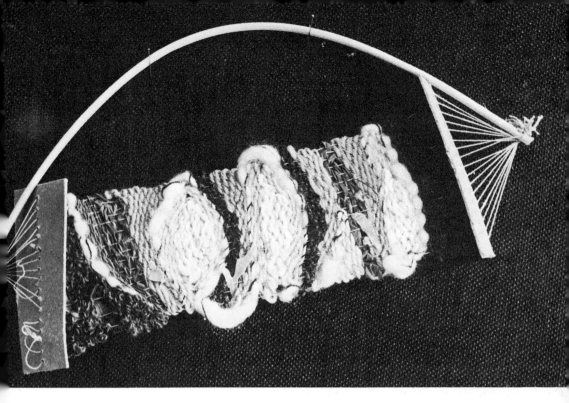

A bow loom made
cane, using pierced
·d to space the warp

can be made by arranging the warp threads in different colours,
alternating single yarns of contrasting colour to make horizontal
stripes or groups of two or more yarns in contrasting colours to
make vertical stripes. The weft can be laid in with a heavy needle,
or with a small stick shuttle which is also used to beat the weft
down firmly.

There are several variations on the bow loom. The tension can
be held by tying two sticks across the bow and winding the warp
over them (fig. 51). This makes a warp on both sides of the frame
which, when woven, forms a tube from which a small bag can be

A bow loom made
ane and dowel rod

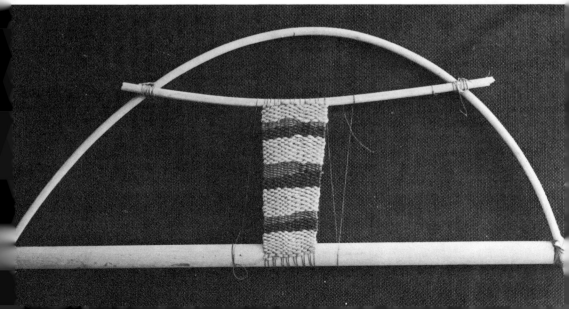

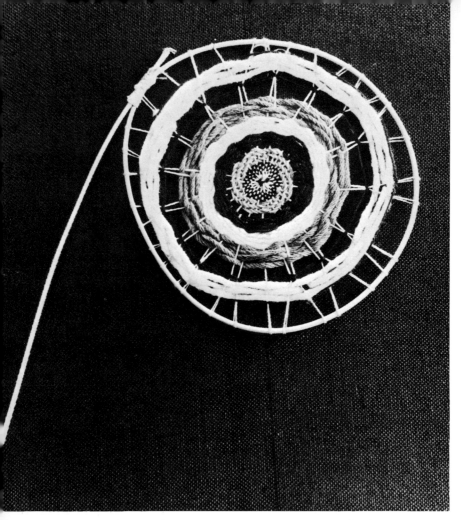

52 A round loom made from cane; the weaving is coarser at the rim

made. To make a round loom from one stick, use flexible material such as cane, willow or young twigs bent into a circle and held in position with string binding, and tie the warp across the diameter (fig. 52). This poses interesting problems, as the texture in the centre, where the warp threads are closer together, will be firmer than that woven on the outer edge. The work may be treated very freely, the stretched yarns used merely as a framework to create internal structures. The finished work can be cut from the frame and the warp ends knotted together in a fringe, or the frame itself may be used as part of the structure. The use of a flexible stick may be extended to other shapes (fig. 53) and many decorative ideas can evolve from the shapes formed in this way. This is an excellent method of introducing weaving to young children.

Two-stick looms used in ancient times are still in common use all over the contemporary world, and can vary from a light structure to a very heavy one. A continuous warp is stretched between parallel sticks, either by winding it first and then inserting the

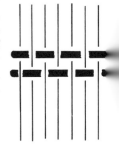

54 Shed sticks

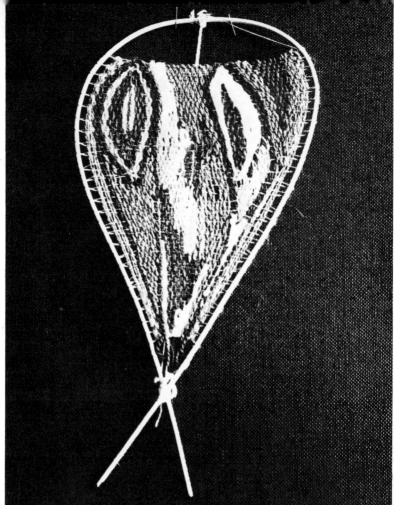

53 Here the curved weft takes the shape of the cane frame, which is held in position by a piece of yarn bound round the joined ends

sticks, or by securing the sticks and passing the yarn between them. The order is kept by means of shed sticks (fig. 54). One end of the warp is secured to an immovable object (a tree, post, radiator, etc.) while a strap or thick yarn is attached to the other end and passed round the weaver's back, and the tension is held by the weaver leaning backwards. This is called a back-strap loom (fig. 55). For your first experiments it is best to use short warps, but longer pieces of weaving may also be made by rolling up the finished weaving on the stick nearest the body and securing it with another stick lashed to it to prevent it from unrolling. A further refinement is possible by using a rigid heddle; this can either be bought, or improvised by fitting lolly sticks or tongue depressors with a hole in the middle into a frame. The warp threads are passed alternately through a hole and the adjacent slot so that they are raised and lowered every time the heddle is pulled up or pushed down (fig. 56). The heddle is used to space the warp and also to beat down the weft, so the structure of a home-made heddle should be

back strap loom.
end is attached to
id object, the strap
e other end goes
d the weaver's

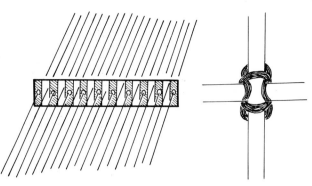

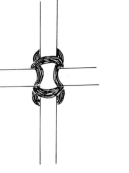

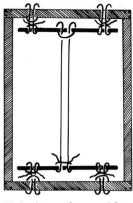

56 Warp threads passed through the holes and slots of a rigid heddle

57 Square lashing

58 A picture frame with two extra end-pieces screwed on to add height; the end sticks are attached to the frame with the split loop and tie shown in fig. 41

quite firm. The spacing of the warp threads will depend on the width of the sticks; bought heddles have about thirteen threads to the inch. From these beginnings it is a short step to the acquisition of a rigid heddle loom with rollers, longer warps, and more elaborate methods of weaving.

Using four sticks is nearer to the form of a conventional loom, and here it is important to use the right type of stick – neither too smooth or slippery, nor too thin or the structure will not be firm. The corners must be bound very tightly together with square lashing (fig. 57), to prevent movement and provide a strong, sturdy frame. The warp can be bound directly round the frame, or sticks can be attached as shown in fig. 58 so that the finished piece can be removed easily. These frames can be made from waste wood, branches etc.; they are flat and therefore easily stored, and are fairly light and easy to move about. The idea can be varied by using found materials, unwanted deck chairs or picture frames, iron bed frames (single size) and so on, but remember that the corners may have to be strengthened with angle brackets to take the strain.

Another easy way to weave is to use headless nails 2–3 cm (1 in) long, driven at intervals into the ends of a frame (fig. 59) or round the perimeter of a circular shape such as a hoop. The warp is wound backwards and forwards round the nails. There may be problems with tension here, as the nails tend to bend as the weaving tightens. As the weaving will have to be taken right up to the loops round the nails, you may find it difficult to pass the weft through the warp for the last few rows, though a needle can be used at this stage. An old bicycle wheel may also be used, the rim providing a permanent frame, the warp passing through the spoke holes; the wheel should be sandpapered and painted before the warp is put on. Nails or pins can be driven into a board in any shape you choose and warp threads wound round them, providing a structure in which the weft is free to take the direction of the shape (fig. 60); in Eastern European countries such as Russia and Czechoslovakia, charming figures in linen thread are made by this method.

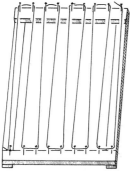

59 The warp wound round nails driven into a frame

60 Circular weaving on nails. For this piece the length of the nails was varied to give a slightly curved surface to the weaving. The design is divided into four sections representing the seasons

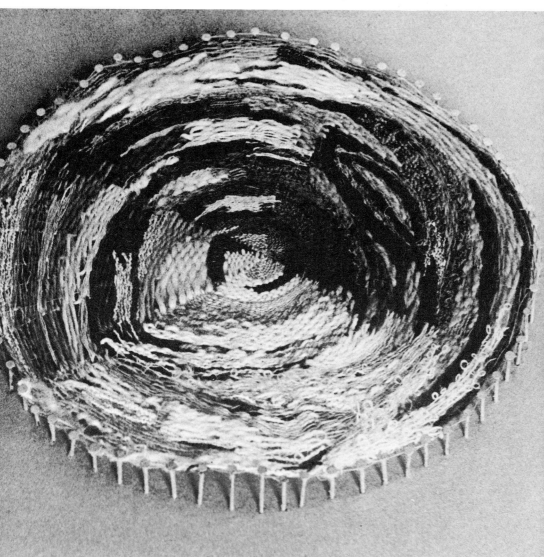

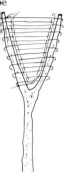

Pieces may be woven on a forked stick, leaving the weaving on the stick if it is to be used as a decorative structure. The warp is wrapped round the forked part and the weft runs in the same direction as the 'handle' (fig. 61). There could also be two faces on which separate pieces could be woven and then cut off, or the two faces could be used in a decorative, three-dimensional way. The same idea may also be used with three sticks lashed together, letting the triangular form influence the direction of the weave (fig. 62). Different coloured yarns simply wrapped round the frame will form interesting three-dimensional patterns of shape and colour (fig. 63).

All these ideas could be used with a group of beginners, either as an introduction to weaving or as an end in themselves, and using the slightly more elaborate pieces of equipment to develop early experiments with card weaving.

63 Coloured yarns wrapped round a frame; the interest lies in the interchange of colour and the shapes made by the space between the yarns

5 Dyeing

Natural dyes

Before 1856 when the research chemist, W. H. Perkin, discovered how to make a synthetic dye from coal tar, all dye came from natural substances. Leaves, flowers, plants, roots, bark, lichens, berries, beetles and shellfish all yield colours which were applied to yarn and cloth. Although natural dyes have been superseded in commercial use by chemical dyes, it is still possible to extract dyes in the traditional way. Very few dyestuffs are substantive, that is, yielding a colour which is fast without the addition of a chemical called a mordant (from the Latin *mordere*, to bite – the ancients believed that it bit into the fibre, causing holes in the surface which held the colour). A mordant creates a chemical affinity between the fibre and the dyestuff, which makes the dye colour the cloth permanently. The usual mordants are alum, iron, tin, chrome and occasionally copper.

Experiments can be made with some of the common plants; even in towns nettles, dock, privet and onion skins will be available and can be used at home or in school or college. The following method yields the maximum result for the minimum of effort. You will need some form of heating such as a gas ring or an electric hot plate; an enamel basin or large pan; several screw-top jars, and a pair of rubber gloves. Chop up the dyestuff into small pieces and place it in the jars with a small quantity of washed fleece or some lengths of woollen yarn. (Wool is the best fibre to use as it has the greatest affinity with natural dyestuffs and the colours will be deeper than if used on cotton or linen. White knitting wool will do, or the first experiments with spinning would be excellent.) Sprinkle a small quantity of alum into each jar, fill them with water and screw on the lids to prevent spilling. Place the jars in the pan with enough water to come half way up the sides, and heat the water to boiling point. Keep it simmering for about an hour, taking care to top up the water as it evaporates, by which time the material should be dyed. The water will not evaporate from the covered jars, and if they are left to cool overnight the colour will have developed even more by the next day. If different chemicals are used with the same dyestuffs you will find that the colours will change, sometimes only in shade but sometimes, particularly with an iron mordant, quite drastically. When the material is removed from the dye it must be rinsed thoroughly and, after drying, it can either be mounted on a chart or the fleece can be spun into a piece of yarn.

In these first attempts the process is easy enough to be really experimental, especially as eight or more jars can be heated at the same time. All sorts of garden plants and fruits can be used in a spirit of enquiry, though not all of them will yield either a colour or a fast dye. In the rinsing process it will be found that small fragments of the dyestuff tend to adhere to the material and for this reason, when dyeing larger quantities, the dyestuff should be loosely tied in muslin so that it will yield colour without becoming entangled in the wool.

For more serious attempts at dyeing larger quantities of wool a different method is used, described below; the wool is first mordanted, and then kept in a damp state overnight before simmering in the dyebath. The usual proportions are equal weights of dyestuff and wool, with the appropriate quantity of whichever mordant you are using.

Mordants

The chief mordants are: alum (potassium aluminium sulphate), tin (stannous chloride), iron (ferrous sulphate), chrome (bichromate of potash). They come in crystal or powdered form, and are usually combined with cream of tartar to brighten the wool and make the dyeing more even. Be careful not to use any of them to excess, or they may make the fibres harsh.

Quantities for 500 grammes (1 lb) of wool
with 500 grammes (1 lb) of dyestuff

alum	85–110 grammes (3–4 oz)	
tin	14 grammes ($\frac{1}{2}$ oz)	with $\frac{1}{2}$ teaspoon
iron	14 grammes ($\frac{1}{2}$ oz)	cream of tartar
chrome	14 grammes ($\frac{1}{2}$ oz) or less	

Quantities for 25 grammes (1 oz) of wool
with 25 grammes (1 oz) of dyestuff

alum	1 teaspoon	
tin	$\frac{1}{8}$ teaspoon	with a pinch of
iron	$\frac{1}{8}$ teaspoon	cream of tartar
chrome	$\frac{1}{8}$ teaspoon	

A set of measuring spoons is useful for getting the quantities accurate; the smallest measure can easily be halved to give $\frac{1}{8}$ teaspoon.

Dissolve the mordant in enough water to cover the wool and bring the solution gradually to the boil, adding the washed wool when the water is warm. If the wool is skeined, it should be tied with figure-of-eight ties as shown in fig. 33, page 48, to avoid tangling when it is unwound. Simmer at boiling point for one hour (three-quarters is enough for finer wools). The wool can then be dyed immediately, but it is better left damp in a plastic bag overnight or for up to two or three days, to allow the mordant to penetrate the fibre more thoroughly.

The dyeing can be carried out in one of several ways. The wool may be mordanted, as above, and then dyed, without having been

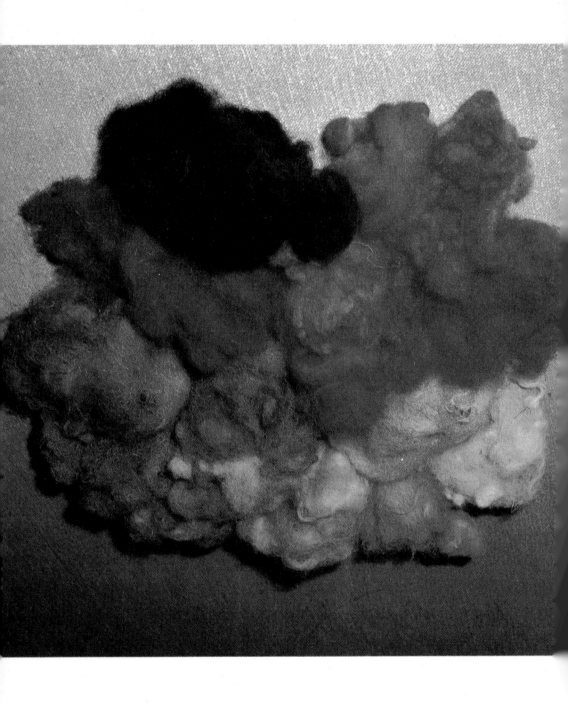

64 A collection of vegetable-dyed fleece; a student's experiment, using roots, flowers, leaves and fruits

rinsed; or the dyestuff may be added with the wool during mordanting, and then boiled for the required time; or sometimes the mordant is added after dyeing. For the first method, add the dyestuff to the water and simmer until the colour is released; the time will vary according to the dyestuff. Dyestuffs made from solid matter should be tied in muslin, or the liquid can be strained off after simmering. Then add the wool to the dyebath, bring it to the boil, and simmer until it reaches the required shade (usually about an hour), after which it should be left in the bath to get cold, allowing it to take up the dye as it does so. Beginners will achieve better results with fleece than with yarn as any unevenness in dyeing will not matter so much, though this can be prevented by gentle stirring during the dyeing. Vegetable dyes are quite difficult to use if a very even colour is required, as the wool should be moved about in the dyebath sufficiently to distribute the dye evenly but not so much as to tangle the skeins or felt the fleece.

Among the natural dyestuffs which are substantive (that is, not requiring a mordant) are those obtained from lichens. Lichens are slow-growing plants found on stones, walls and trees in damp climates; they should not be collected indiscriminately, as each tiny plant takes years to grow. Again, equal weights of wool and dyestuff are required. The lichen must be simmered for several hours and allowed to get cold. The next day the wetted wool is boiled in the liquid until it acquires the right depth of colour. Another method is to bring lichen and wool to the boil together, simmer for several hours, and leave to cool overnight. Cudbear is a substance derived from lichens, which can be obtained in powdered form; a tablespoonful used with wool previously mordanted with alum will produce a beautiful purple, and in this case the dyeing takes only about half an hour.

There is a wide variety of plants which will give a fast colour, and half the interest in vegetable dyeing is in collecting or growing these plants. Most of them can be found growing wild, but many of them can be cultivated in the garden.

A chart of common dye plants

YELLOWS

Barberry	Heather	Fustic
Birch bark	Lichen	Cutch
Bracken	Ling	Persian berries
Broom	Marigold	Weld
Dog Mercury	Nettle	
Dyer's Greenwood	Onion skin	
Golden Rod	Privet	
Gorse	Ragwort	

GREENS

Bracken	Horsetail	Fustic
Broom	Privet	
Buckthorn	Reeds	

BROWNS

Birch bark	Onion skin	Cutch
Blackberry	Pine cones	Fustic
Lichen	Walnut	Logwood
Oak		Madder

BLACK

Blackberry	Iris	Logwood
Dock root	Meadowsweet	
Elder	Walnut	

REDS

Bedstraw	Lichen	Cochineal
Blackberry	St John's Wort	Kermes
	Madder	Redwood

BLUES

Blackberry	Sloe	Indigo
Dog Mercury	Whortleberry	Logwood

ORANGE

Lichen	Flavine	Turmeric
Onion skin	Fustic	
Weld	Madder	

PURPLES

Birch bark	Cudbear	Cochineal
Damson	Logwood	
Elder	Orchil	
Potentilla		

The chart shows several dyestuffs as producing different colours, due to the use of different mordants. In general an iron mordant darkens the colour, and in some cases changes it completely, while the others tend to change less drastically, i.e. from yellow to orange, or red to red-brown. If experiments are made with small quantities by the jam-jar method before going on to dye in bulk, a chart could be built up of the colours obtained by varying the mordant. Remember, too, that the dye obtained from plants is not constant, depending on the time of year, the part of the plant used, and whether it is fresh or dried.

Synthetic dyes

The history of dyeing with synthetics began with an accident. In trying to produce synthetic quinine W. H. Perkin, then a chemistry student, produced a substance from coal tar which dyed silk purple. This substance, called Perkin's Mauveine, started a chain of new discoveries which led to the development of a complex modern dyeing industry. Alizarin and azo dyes were next invented, covering a wide range of dyestuffs which dyed wool, cotton, linen and silk very successfully. Later vat dyes were invented and produced a very fast dye. The invention of rayons caused initial difficulty in dyeing, as acetate rayon in particular is difficult to dye by the normal processes, and a wide new range of dyestuffs was invented to dye the fibre. The great advantage of these dyestuffs is that they are used in powder form, a small amount of powder producing a large amount of colour. Direct dyes were used with salt on cottons, and acid dyes were used in a solution of acid for wool, so that their application simply required boiling for a specified time to fix the dyestuff on to the fibre. The industrial process is more complicated, but household dyes were made available, so that home dyeing became possible by the addition of salt for cottons and linens, and vinegar for wools and silks. The dyes were not as fast as the commercial process, but were very popular.

In 1955, a hundred years after the invention of the first synthetic dye, another big breakthrough took place with the invention of reactive dyes. Previously the dyestuff had been fixed by boiling to make it adhere to the surface of the fibre, so that, in simple terms, $A+B = AB$, when A is the fibre, and B the dyestuff. The reactive dyes produced a change in the chemical structure of the fibre so that $A+B$ became C, another substance, and the change was irreversible, the dye being extremely fast. These dyes have been made available for home use under the trade name Dylon, and are suitable both for the natural fibres and for nylon and viscose rayon, but having a particular affinity for cellulose they are specifically effective for dyeing cotton. A range is made for cold-water application, and this makes possible a variety of techniques which, especially for schools, were not so suitable when most dyes had to be applied by boiling.

Recipes for dyeing about 500 grammes (1 lb) of yarn or material
These recipes are intended to be used experimentally as a means of developing an eye for colour. First mix a teaspoonful of dye in a glass jar with some warm water, making sure that the dye powder is completely dissolved or the dyeing will be uneven. The fabric or skeined yarn should be washed, rinsed well, and left wet. The dyebath should be made of enamel or stainless steel, and you will need measuring spoons and, ideally, glass rods for stirring, though spoons or sticks will do as long as the dyed sticks are kept away from light colours in subsequent dyeings.

DIRECT DYES – I.C.I. CHLOROZOL AND DURAZOL RANGE FOR COTTONS The dyebath is prepared with one tablespoonful of salt for each 500 grammes (1 lb) of yarn and some of the dye solution in enough water to cover the material. Be very careful, if a pale shade is required, not to use too much dyestuff. The material is entered in the dyebath and brought slowly to the boil, moving it about in the solution to ensure that the dye is penetrating thoroughly and evenly. After simmering for twenty minutes to half an hour the dye should be fixed to the fibre, and the dyed material can be rinsed in cold water to remove any loose dye. If the fabric takes up the dye quickly and the water is clear, the resulting colour may be too pale. More dye solution may be added, taking the material out first and stirring the solution well before putting it back. Some dyes penetrate more evenly than others, and at different temperatures and speeds, and experience will tell how much dye to use to achieve the colour required. Dyestuffs in the same range can be mixed, and as a rough guide to the final colour let a few drops of dye solution fall into a jar of water, holding the clear solution up to the light, or drop a stronger mixture on to a piece of white blotting paper. Remember, too, that the colour on the wet material will be stronger by several shades than when it is dry.

ACID DYES – I.C.I. COOMASSIE AND LISSAMINE RANGE FOR WOOL, SILK AND NYLONS The dyebath is prepared in a similar way to the direct dyebath above, adding three tablespoons of Glauber's Salt (sodium sulphate) and one tablespoonful of 30% dilute sulphuric acid to the solution before the material is entered. Be very careful with the acid, always adding the acid to the water, not the other way round, and if any splashing occurs rinse it off at once, for even at this dilution it can burn the skin and eat away fabric or wood. If you are dubious about this you can buy a weaker solution of the acid and use more of it in proportion. Bring the dye solution to the boil and maintain this for twenty minutes to half an hour. If much dye solution is left in the water, and the shade is still too pale, add a little more acid, remembering to remove the material first. The aim should be to exhaust the dyebath completely until a clear liquid is left.

You may want to dye yarn unevenly in order to have a variety of shades in the same colour. This is particularly useful for yarns being used for tufted rugs, and for certain types of weaving it will give a pleasing variation to the colour without looking like a mistake. There are several methods of achieving this. A small quantity of the dyestuff can be added to the bath initially, and the rest added at various stages during the dyeing, without removing the skeins, and with very little stirring. Small amounts of dry powder can be added to the bath so that a heavy concentration of colour is fixed to small areas, gradually dissolving into the rest of the dye. The material can be crammed into a small dyebath so that it cannot move easily, which will fix the dye more heavily on some areas than others. More dye can be dripped on to the crammed material, and if this is in a related, harmonising shade interesting mixtures of colour can result.

REACTIVE DYES – DYLON RANGE FOR COTTON, LINEN, SILK, WOOL AND VISCOSE RAYON The chemical nature of reactive dyes makes their use more precise than the older dyes. Recipes should be followed exactly or the chemical change cannot take place and the dyestuff will wash out of the fabric.

It is important to wash the yarn or cloth thoroughly before

65 The circular cane which frames this piece of weaving has been left as part of the construction. Yarns are wound at random across it, forming several central points around which the weft is woven

dyeing, so that all dressing is removed. Some natural cotton yarns need boiling in soda for an hour to remove the natural waxes and other impurities from the cellulose. Cloth which has been given a special finish such as crease or shrink resist will not take the dye well, if at all. The dyes, salt and soda solutions should be prepared beforehand, and not mixed together before the yarn is introduced into the bath, or the reaction of the alkali with the dye will take place on its own, and the cloth will emerge very much paler than the intended shade. Dyeing mercerised cotton with reactive dye is particularly successful because it is already treated with alkali. If the recipe is followed properly the dye will be completely fast.

There are two types of reactive dye which are readily available, Dylon Cold Water Dye and Dylon Multipurpose Dye. Small tins are available in local shops and multiple stores and larger tins, which are more economical, are available from Dylon International.

COLD WATER DYES   To dye 250 grammes (8 oz) fabric or yarn: 1 tin (or 10 grammes) dye; $\frac{1}{2}$ litre (1 pint) warm water; 4 tablespoons common salt; 1 tablespoon common soda; $\frac{1}{2}$ litre (1 pint) hot water; 4·5 litres (8 pints) cold water.

Dissolve the dye in the warm water. Mix the salt and soda in the hot water until dissolved. Wet the yarn or fabric, and just before it is ready to be immersed, mix the two solutions with up to eight pints of cold water. Enter the material and dye for half an hour, stirring constantly for the first ten minutes, then at intervals. Rinse thoroughly in running cold water to remove the loose dye, then wash in very hot detergent, rinsing again in cold water before drying. The hot detergent wash is an essential part of the process, and can be varied by immersing the dyed fabric in boiling detergent water and leaving for five minutes or so before rinsing.

MULTIPURPOSE DYES   To dye 250 grammes (8 oz) fabric or yarn: 10 grammes (1 tin) dye; $\frac{1}{2}$ litre (1 pint) boiling water; 4·5 litres (8 pints) hot water; 3 teaspoons salt.

Dissolve the dye in the boiling water and add to the hot water. Enter the yarn and bring to a simmer, adding the salt gradually over a period of twenty minutes, and keeping the water at just under boiling point. Wash in hot detergent before rinsing and drying.

The timing of the dyeing is important, and the final washing in hot detergent completes the process, the colour then being extremely fast. A tin of dye holds $2\frac{1}{2}$ level teaspoons; before any large scale work is attempted, it is wise to experiment with scaled down quantities of dye, salt and soda.

The art of dyeing is more than the application of colour to fabric (see chapter 6). An eye for colour can be developed, and a knowledge of how colour works is of great assistance in working out the shade you need. There are three primary colours, red, blue and yellow, so called because they are not made up of other colours. Each pair of primaries mixed together makes the three secondaries; red and yellow make orange; blue and red make purple; yellow and blue make green. Further mixtures of the secondaries make tertiaries (fig. 66). Colours adjacent to one another on the colour wheel are called harmonies, and those opposite each other are complementaries. Harmonies may be blended together, and if a small quantity of a complementary is used with a mixture of its opposite harmonies the complementary will appear at its maximum brightness. The fun of dyeing is in the mixing of colours to produce something that is individual, and for this reason I prefer acid dyes and direct dyes for this sort of experimentation. By adding small quantities of dye liquor, the colour can be changed by degrees until it is exactly the shade required. It is often said that vegetable dyes are better than the synthetics, because they give softer and more harmonious shades, but it is possible to mix the synthetic dyes to correspond to anything that vegetable dyes can produce, which can be proved by doing an exercise in exact colour matching. This could also be accomplished by using paintings and reproductions in the same way as for yarn mixing (page 49).

The recipes given are simple ones, but it should be realised that dyeing is a very complex and exact science, and to become really knowledgeable you will need a great deal more information and, above all, practice.

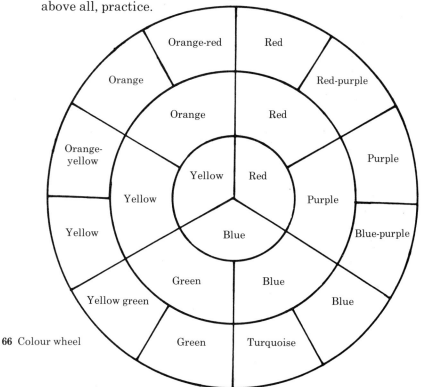

66 Colour wheel

6 Designing in dye

Tie-and-dye

Dyeing has more to it than the application of dyestuff to yarn or fabric, and the art lies in the method by which the dye is applied. Uneven dyeing of yarns has been mentioned, and can be taken a stage further by dyeing warp and weft yarns to form a pattern. In this form of dyeing, sections of the warp are bound very tightly so that when the whole warp is dyed the bound sections resist the colour and form a pattern. To do this, the warp is made in the usual way, and then spread out between sticks, secured to keep it taut. The sections required to resist the dye are then bound together very tightly (fig. 67), and the complete warp is dyed. After drying the warp is untied and put on to the frame or loom. The threads tend to shift about slightly, and this gives a tied-and-dyed warp its characteristic appearance, the pattern having rather blurred edges. Weft yarns can be tie-dyed in a similar way, though it is difficult to place the pattern exactly where it is wanted. The most difficult feat is the mixture of warp and weft tie-dyeing so that the pattern is formed exactly where the resisted part of both warp and weft meet. This form of decoration reaches a very high standard of artistry in Indonesia, India, Peru and Japan, the Okinawan textiles being renowned for it. It is advisable to experiment with very small warps and fairly coarse yarns at first, until the technique is mastered. A random tied-and-dyed effect may be obtained by binding a hank of yarn at intervals. If the size of the hank is slightly larger or smaller than the width of the weaving a repeating pattern may result.

67 Two sections bound warp ready dyeing

The tie-and-dye technique is more commonly applied to fabric than yarn, and this is a fairly easy craft to master if basic rules are strictly followed. This, too, is a resist technique in which the fabric is bound in such a way that the cloth resists the dye at the places where binding occurs. For experiments use old sheets, pillowcases, handkerchiefs etc., which, because they have been washed frequently, are soft and absorbent. A fine fabric will give a better result than a coarse one, so if you are buying new material choose a fine calico; it must be washed thoroughly before use to remove the dressing. Divide your fabric approximately into 30-cm (12-in) squares for initial samples. These may be tied in various ways to produce a pattern, using a variety of strings and hard cotton yarns for tying.

Preparing the material

MARBLING Crumple the fabric roughly in the hand, and tie string tightly in several directions round the resulting bundle. This gives a randomly textured background (fig. 68).

68 Marbling; the f[...] is bunched up an[...] tightly

74

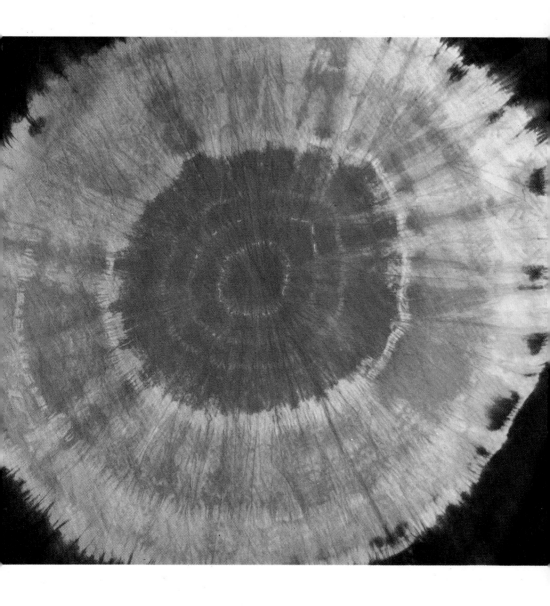

69 Tied-and-dyed fabric. The interest of this large circular design lies in the combination of brilliant colours

CIRCLES Lift a point in the centre of the material with one hand, and fold it down to the corners through the other hand. Start binding about an inch below the point, and continue in sections until the edges of the sample are reached. This will produce a textured circle (fig. 70). Small stones, buttons, etc. may also be used for tying circular shapes.

PLEATING Fold the material like a concertina, binding the resulting strip at intervals. The dye will be absorbed into the ridges of the pleat, making a striped material with wider textured stripes across it (fig. 71).

FOLDING Fold the material diagonally twice, then pleat and bind it; or fold it in half, then in half again, then pleat and bind it. These two methods make a very strong pattern which is most attractive.

The golden rule is to tie tightly enough. I have often told students that if their fingers blister in the process this is good, as it proves that they are pulling the string adequately! It does, in fact, take that kind of strong pull to bind strongly enough to prevent the dye seeping underneath, and the solution is either to protect the fingers with a piece of sticking plaster, or to wind the yarn round a piece of wood, or a pencil, to pull against. It is also essential to make the binding wide enough, as allowance has to be made for seepage, and if the string is given only one or two turns a very thin line will result, without much texture. Experiment will soon reveal errors : too loose a tie will result in very little pattern appearing, while too tight, or too extensive a tie will result in very little dye penetrating at all. Press the binding with your fingers, and if it gives to the touch it is too loose. There are many ways of experimenting with these four simple techniques, for many different methods of folding and binding are possible even within these limits. There are other ways, too, of resisting the dye, by using rubber bands, clothes pegs, bulldog clips etc., and this is all part of the fun of experimenting.

70 Circles; two cir will form where cloth is bound, and background will textured

71 Pleating; the will be strongest at folds and two text stripes will be for by the binding

Dyeing
Rubber gloves are even more essential for tie-and-dye than for ordinary dyeing, as all the dye solutions are much stronger.

COLD WATER DYES 1 tin or two level teaspoons dye; 4 tablespoons salt; 1 tablespoon soda; $\frac{1}{2}$ litre (1 pint) warm water; $\frac{1}{2}$ litre (1 pint) hot water.

Dissolve the dye in the warm water, and the soda and salt in the hot water. When both are cool, and the sample is tied, mix the solutions together; this gives a strong dye solution. The sample is immersed, either wet or dry, and dyed for half an hour to one hour, stirring for the first ten minutes, then at intervals. If the sample is wet before entering, this will impede the penetration of the dye as the cotton ties will shrink and tighten when wet. The sample must be thoroughly rinsed before and after untying; when removing the ties, make sure that you do not cut the fabric. A final hot wash in detergent will help set the colour, making it fast. Several samples may be immersed at the same time, and variation can be given by having several colours on the go and immersing only a part of each tied sample, so that the centres of circles can be a different colour from the rest; and by bending long pleated samples the ends can be different from the middle. Interesting effects are produced when the colours blend into one another, because dyes have differing rates of capillary attraction and mixtures can separate into their components, giving unexpected bonus effects. If the dyed strings used for tying are re-used without washing, these can often create extra colour mixtures which are entirely individual. I once tied circles round some old red wooden buttons and the dye from them bled on to the material, giving just enough red to make a focal point in the design. More complicated effects are achieved when designs are untied and re-tied in different places, which is when a knowledge of colour mixing is essential.

DIRECT DYES   1 level teaspoon dye; 1 tablespoon salt; 1–1½ litres (2–3 pints) water. Dissolve the dye in a little warm water, add the rest of the water and bring the solution to the boil, adding the salt when it is boiling. Then immerse the tied fabric in the boiling solution. These dyes are easier to use in some respects than the cold water dyes, as although the dye liquor has to be boiled, the fabric is immersed for a very short time. In normal dyeing the aim is to achieve an even colour and the dye is carefully mixed, the solution being brought slowly to the boil. Here, the process is just the opposite. The dye solution is brought to the boil, and the tied bundle boiled for three to five minutes only, according to the thickness of the fabric and how tightly it is tied. Again, experiment with the 30-cm (12-in) squares, using only enough dye liquor to cover the sample. If you want to dye part of it only, it can be suspended from string tied across the top of the pan, but be careful not to let the gas flame flare up the side of the pan. Rinse before and after the sample is untied, and dry. Do not iron while damp, or spotting may occur. The best way to remove the creases is to smooth out the wet sample on a window, a formica table top, or on the side of the bath. The moisture evaporates quickly and the creases disappear much more easily than if the fabric is ironed after drying. Any staining left behind can be removed with bleach.

ACID DYES   Silk and wool may be tied-and-dyed in the same way as with the direct dyes, using similar proportions of dye, acid and alkali as in the ordinary recipe, but with less water. The beginner, however, is recommended to experiment with the cotton materials first, as fine wool and silk are too expensive to risk spoiling.

Tie-and-dye techniques are found in very many parts of the world, including India, Africa, Thailand, Indonesia, Malaysia, China, Japan, and historically in America, Mexico, Guatemala and Peru. Very complex patterns appear when a fabric is tied-and-dyed, then untied and re-tied in a different place and dyed again, repeating the process several times. The knowledge of how colours will combine to produce the desired result comes from long experience in using a comparatively small range of colours and the willingness to tie literally hundreds of ties to achieve some of the patterns. The process is slow and meticulous, but attractive patterns may still be perfected by the less complicated methods.

As tie-and-dye produces a pattern which cannot be exactly repeated the best results are obtained when the pattern is tied to fit into a certain shape. For example, rather than make a garment out of a length of tied-and-dyed material, the garment should be cut out and the pattern applied to the individual pieces. If circles are being used, always mark out lightly in pencil where the centres are to come, for once the first circle is tied the fabric is so distorted that it is difficult to see where the others should go. If a large area is being attempted in a folded technique it is useful to pencil exactly where a diagonal should go, especially if a rectangle rather than a square is used. The pleat can then be centred on the pencil line, and an accurate diagonal is kept. By using accurate diagonal pleats very well designed bedspreads can be made from sheets, using several colours. Although it is to a certain extent a random technique, tie-and-dye can be controlled and designed to make individual articles of dress, toys, and decorative objects.

If tie-and-dye is used in schools, preparation should be done well in advance, using plenty of newspaper to cover tables, and not forgetting rubber gloves for the teacher and sticking plaster for sore fingers. With smaller children tying is best done in groups, and the ties should be checked. Bowls, jam jars and dyes should be prepared beforehand; and name tags can be attached by long strings to the tied samples, which can then be placed in the bowl of dye and pushed under by the teacher wearing rubber gloves. If this is timed for just before the mid-morning break the samples could stay in until after lunch, when the teacher could prepare them for the afternoon if there is no sink in the classroom. The rinsed samples can then be placed on well-covered desks, with the string cut so that they can be untied easily. This method can be used with quite young children as well as with older ones, and can be carried out in fairly large groups as well as small ones. It does help if there is running water in the classroom, but if the operation is well planned this is not absolutely necessary. Children working with tie-and-dye for the first time are quite delighted when a pattern emerges from their soggy bundle. The samples can be dried on the windows where everyone can see them, and can be used for table mats and small cushions, etc., or they can be sewn together to make a large curtain or hanging. A group effort on a large piece of material could also be attempted, and older students may like to try dresses or shirts. Other group projects could be carried out in connection with a school play, using the technique to design costumes and curtains.

72 Batik. A simple repeating design in two colours; the wax was applied with a paint brush

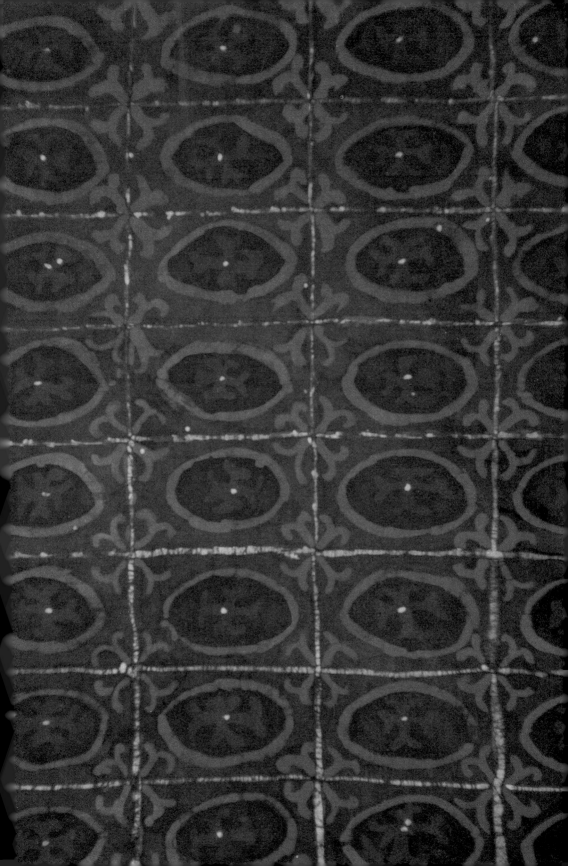

Batik

Batik is a Malaysian word meaning to design by painting or tracing, and the technique consists of painting a design on to fabric with hot wax or starch paste to exclude the dye. It was originally brought to Europe, and subsequently to America, by the early Dutch traders.

Again, small cotton samples should be made, using white or light-coloured fabric. To keep the fabric taut while the wax is applied, pin, staple or tape the edges over a wooden or cardboard box, or stretch it across the space between two tables; it could also be taped to several layers of paper, though this is less effective. Beeswax, paraffin wax, melted candles or a mixture of these can be used. Heat the wax in a small pan placed in a larger pan of water, so that the wax cannot ignite. When the wax is hot, the first layer of the design is painted on to the stretched fabric, making sure that it penetrates right through the fabric. If the wax cools on the surface it is likely to be brushed off, and the dye will penetrate where it is not wanted. When the wax is cold, place the fabric in a cold water dye solution, using a pale shade for the first dipping, as more colour will be added for the second part of the design. After carefully rinsing and drying, more wax is painted on and the sample is dipped again into a darker dye. This will produce three colours, the white or pale ground material, the first colour, and a mixture of the first and second colours. If areas of the second colour are required, the whole sample will have to be cleaned of wax and then rewaxed. It is clear, therefore, that a very careful consideration of colour is important, as each separate waxing and dipping will produce a colour mixture. A safe way to be sure of the result would be to use successively darker shades of the same colour, or shades closely related on the colour wheel. It is difficult to see how the design is progressing as the fabric is gradually covered by successive layers of wax, though if it is held up to the light the colours will show through the translucent wax.

If the design is to be pictorial, it may be drawn lightly on the material first; or a purely random use of colour related to the technique may be attempted. Hot wax can be dribbled and dropped from a lighted candle; experiments with bold brush strokes could be attempted; stencilled shapes could be made, and the wax applied within the shape; a tjanting tool, which holds hot wax in a copper container with a spout, makes a very fine line for more delicate effects. The important thing to remember is to keep the wax hot enough to penetrate the cloth thoroughly, painting on the back as well if necessary. The pan used for dyeing should be shallow, and preferably large enough to take the whole piece laid flat. Enamel meat tins, butchers' and photographers' trays are all good. They are not, however, essential as part of the unique effect of batik is the way the dye seeps through cracks in the wax, and this effect may be deliberately introduced by folding or crushing the material in a small container. The wax will, in any case, tend to crack slightly when the fabric is moved about in the pan, and there may also be bonus colour effects due to seepage and the different rates of capillary attraction, as in tie-and-dye. The Dylon cold-water dyes are, of course, ideal for batik work.

After the last waxing and drying, scrape off as much wax as possible with a blunt knife, and keep it for re-use. Then immerse the cloth in very hot water, to melt off the wax which has soaked into the fabric. This wax may also be kept, as it hardens as the water cools. The cloth must then be washed in a very hot detergent solution, several times if necessary, until all the remaining wax is removed. If it is not removed completely the cloth will be stiff, and may develop a dark line round the shapes.

A thick paste of flour and water or a stiff wallpaper paste may also be used for batik, and this is easier to remove. The effect, however, is slightly different, as the paste does not have the brittle quality of wax. It is suitable for school use where the heating of wax may be dangerous, and the same preparations should be made as for tie-and-dye, with plenty of paper and the dyes, alkali and pastes already mixed beforehand. Another reason why paste may be more suitable for school use is that caretakers do not usually take kindly to having the sinks constantly blocked with wax! This is, in fact, a considerable hazard in batik work, and can only be avoided by extreme care and the use of plenty of hot detergent water while working, as once the wax hardens in the pipe it is a major operation to unblock it.

Batik is a suitable technique both for dress fabric and for decorative uses. Again, the individual effect is achieved by designing into the shape of the garment after it is cut out, rather than designing in the length. Batik pictures show to great advantage if they are given a box mounting, lit from behind, when the effect will be similar to stained glass.

Fabric printing
Although perhaps the most sophisticated of all the dyeing techniques, printing on fabric can, at least in its simpler forms, be practised successfully at all levels of attainment, and by all ages. A new development in reactive dyes, called craft dyes and put out by the British firm of Reeves, simplifies all the printing processes, and can even be used in a different form for tie-and-dye. These dyes come in a range of eight colours, plus black, and what is called an extender can be mixed with the colours to make paler shades. The colours can, of course, be mixed together. The dye is used direct from the container, undiluted, and can even be mixed directly on the fabric. Once the design is dry, a fixing solution is spread over the cloth, which is then rolled up and enclosed in a polythene bag for at least four hours to dry slowly. The fabric is then washed and rinsed thoroughly until no more colour runs out, when it can be dried in the air, and ironed in the usual way. This process is of such simplicity compared with other processes that it is to be

recommended for the beginner, and for classroom use.

Printed fabrics are fabrics to which dyestuff is applied in a thickened form, so that it adheres to the surface of the fabric without spreading outside the confines of the pattern. The simplest way of applying the dye paste is by painting it on to the fabric with a brush. This gives great freedom in use, and the effect is virtually that of a painting. An exact pattern repeat is not, however, possible by this process, and can only be achieved by using a block or a stencil to apply the dye, or by screen printing. Simple blocks can be made from potatoes, corks, lino, rubber, and from textured objects such as plastic brushes, corrugated cardboard and hair rollers. Blocks made from string glued on to a piece of wood can also be used. The patterns produced are suitable for small repeats over the area of the fabric or, as before, for decorating specific areas or the cut-out pieces of a garment. Potato blocks are very easy to make; the potato is hard enough to hold the shape but soft enough to cut quickly, and the two halves of the potato present a smooth, compact surface from which to cut the shape (fig. 73). The pattern is cut into the block so that the shape stands out from the surrounding area, and the block is then dipped into the dye and applied to the fabric. A piece of sponge foam inserted into a small container such as a margarine tub and then spread with dye makes a good pad to hold the dye. The sample to be printed should be placed on a slightly padded surface on which it can be stretched out flat and held with pins or adhesive tape; tables padded with newspaper and covered with an old plastic cloth make an adequate printing surface. To avoid smudging it is advisable not to move the samples before they are dry. If a pattern is to be repeated over a large area, the fabric should be marked out in squares, either lightly with a pencil or with thread secured to the edges with adhesive tape.

73 A potato block to produce a circular design

Stencils made of thin card can also be used, and could be printed in conjunction with block prints. The dye is applied with a firm pad made of cloth or foam rubber or with a special stencilling brush.

Stencilling leads on to screen printing, which can be a very complicated process using different screens for the super-imposition of several colours. There is, however, a much easier way for first attempts. A flat frame is needed, and can be improvised from a picture frame provided it is not warped; it is advisable to start with a small frame which will be easier to control. A piece of organdie large enough to extend beyond the side of the frame is used for the screen. Secure one end to the outside edge of the frame with drawing pins (thumb tacks) or staples, and then stretch it over the frame and secure it to the opposite edge, making sure that the threads of the fabric are parallel to the sides of the frame. The fabric must be stretched very tightly and evenly across the whole area. The other two sides are then pinned in the same way. The screen must then be masked with strips of brown adhesive paper applied to the inside of the frame,

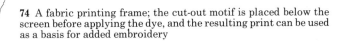

74 A fabric printing frame; the cut-out motif is placed below the screen before applying the dye, and the resulting print can be used as a basis for added embroidery

extending about 5 cm (2 ins) over the organdie and up the sides of the frame and evenly placed to form a rectangular shape.

In screen printing the dye is not applied direct but penetrates through the organdie to the fabric beneath. There are two easy ways of making a pattern, both based on stencils. Cut the required shape out of paper, and place it on the fabric below the screen (fig. 74). Spread the dye over one end of the screen, being careful not to use too much, and pull it evenly over the surface to the other end with a squeegee, which is a thick piece of rubber inserted between two strips of wood. A squeegee can be improvised from strong card, draught excluders, old plastic rulers and so on, as long as there is a straight edge and the strip is reasonably flexible. When the screen is lifted, the shape will be outlined by the surrounding printed area. The reverse of this process is to cut out the shape from a large piece of cartridge paper and pin or staple this as smoothly as possible over the outside of the screen. The dye is applied as before, and this time the cut-out shape will be printed while the surrounding area is left clear. This method is not suitable for the reproduction of a large number of prints, or for very fine and detailed work, but where, say, a set of table mats or cushion covers are required, it is a quick way of approaching the technique. The prints could also be used as a starting point for the addition of embroidery, or in combination with tied-and-dyed fabric.

Prints should first be tried out on old pieces of fabric, so that the amount of dye necessary can be gauged. Do not squeeze too much dye through the screen, or it will flood and give a blurred outline. A design may be varied by turning it round in different directions, or printing in different colours. This is easier to achieve with the stamped type of print, such as a potato print, as the old dye has to be washed off the screen each time the colour is changed. Use cold running water, scrubbing the screen with a soft brush, before the dye has had time to dry. Blot the screen with kitchen paper, holding it against the light to see whether any dye is still blocking the mesh. The masking paper may be replaced if it comes away.

Bold shapes are suitable for your first designs; more refined shapes become possible with the use of an adhesive sheet such as Pro-film from which the design is cut away with a craft knife, and a more delicate effect can be obtained. At first, however, concentrate on making an even print with solid colour and clean edges, before any complex designs are attempted. This applies to first attempts at designing printed fabrics in the classroom, where all the rules about the preparation of tables, dyes etc. still apply. It is easier for children to work in pairs at first, one holding the screen steady while the other moves the squeegee, taking great care to lift the screen cleanly to avoid smudged edges. As washing the screens is important, there must be access to running water.

7 The educational value of textiles

There are many ways of extending the exploration of textile ideas in schools and colleges, which can be varied according to the age of the children or students.

Children's interest may be stimulated by the examination of their own clothes, and they are fascinated by the processes of weaving and spinning and always eager to 'have a go'. Several fairy tales have spinning as a theme, and young children respond well to stories like *Rumpelstiltskin*, particularly when they have had direct experience of handling fleece and a spindle. They also enjoy investigating the properties of yarn as described in chapter 2, and these exercises can be followed by discussions which in turn can lead on to writing about the sensations of touch, sight and smell and the way yarns have a life of their own which makes them form the shapes they assume naturally. Counting the number of plies in a yarn or the threads in very loosely woven hessian (burlap) can be used for a variety of simple number exercises. Fabric collage and the beginnings of embroidery can be explored in a creative way, and the experimental knitted shapes described on pages 32–3 are fun for children and also teach the creative combination of thread and needle; if they are allowed to evolve their own number system and work on it the counting involved and the recording of it will be instructive as well as creative. The ideas given in chapter 4 for weaving on card and on primitive looms could be used in schools, again either as an end in themselves or as a means of introducing weaving to a class, and the first experiments on cards could be developed on the various different pieces of equipment. Activities involving writing and painting should always be used to support and elaborate any textile exercises, emphasising the tactile and visual qualities of the material.

Animals which produce textile fibres can be talked about, and silkworms and even rabbits could be kept in suitable circumstances. Nature study could include the collection of fleece from the hedgerows, in a sheep farming district, for dyeing, spinning and weaving with simple equipment. Wild plants could be collected to make natural dyes, or children could grow plants at home or in the school garden, and a group could take the whole process through dyeing to spinning and weaving. This would lead to a greater appreciation of what was involved before synthetic dyes were invented and dyeing became possible by simply mixing a commercially prepared powder with water and chemicals.

Older children can pursue many topics in relation to textiles as well as working with them as an art and craft activity. The making of yarn and cloth is bound up very closely with history and

5-9
Photographs of a pro-
ject on wool carried
out with six-year-old
children

The children visit
the sheep and feel the
fleece

geography, going back to Ancient Greece and Egypt, with the
medieval wool trade and the Industrial Revolution forming an
important part of European history. The English language
contains many textile terms, such as *wool-gathering* to describe
an absent-minded person; *heckling*, one of the 'agonies' of flax;
spinster, the unmarried woman who did the spinning; *dyed-in-
the-wool*, from the most penetrating way of dyeing, i.e.
unalterable; *born to the purple*, of royal blood, derived from the
Tyrian purple used only by royalty in ancient times; *shuttle service*,
from the to-and-fro movement of the weaving shuttle; *on
tenterhooks*, from the time when cloth was stretched on them
to dry; and to *unravel* a mystery. Many names, too, like Dyer,
Webster, Packer and Fuller, have origins in the textile trade, while
English inn names like The Woolpack or The Drover's Arms
indicate an old wool route used when sheep and cattle were driven
many miles on foot to market. Literature is full of textile allusion;
Shakespeare's plays, for example, and the Bible contain many

76 A painting of t[he]
princess who spun

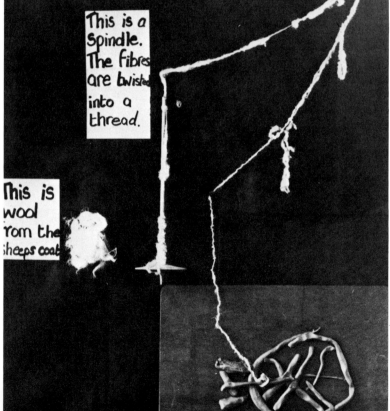

This is a
Spindle.
The fibres
are twisted
into a
thread.

This is
wool
from the
sheeps coat

77 and 78
Part of the wall di[s]
lay. The sheep colla[r]
was made from r[aw]
fleece, and the ya[rn]
was spun by the chi[ld]
ren

Mrs Seagroatt came to show us how to spin.

Here is the sheep

references to weaving, dyeing and spinning which enrich the language and the meaning of the text.

For students there is a rich field of sociological investigation in the way textiles have affected the lives of workers through the ages, from the formation of the early Guilds, through the employment of child labour, to the introduction of aniline dyes to peasant weavers in more recent times which has changed their way of life in many countries. Some of these events have been recorded in folk song and a rewarding group exercise could be the compilation of a folk documentary on these and similar lines. Having compiled one myself, I have experienced the interest kindled by the extended knowledge of a subject which comes with the sort of reading that must be done to condense facts into a paragraph. Dyeing with both natural and synthetic dyes has a scientific basis, and many experiments could be made on the properties of dyes, including the testing of yarns for their fibre content. A rural science department could rear animals such as sheep, goats and angora rabbits which produce a textile fibre. Textile and dye plants could also be grown, either outside, or in the greenhouse where even some of the tropical plants might be attempted.

The photographs in figs. 75–9 show a session with some six-year-old children. They were taken to the rural science department of a local college of education where they were introduced to the sheep. They had never been close to one before, and were astonished at how greasy the wool felt. When they went back to school they described the visit in words and pictures, and the spinning of fleece was demonstrated on a hand spindle and on a spinning wheel. Later they were told the story of the princess who could spin gold from straw and clay, and they painted pictures and modelled the spinning wheel in plasticine. The results were made into a wall display. The children were not, on the whole, of more than average ability, but they responded enthusiastically to the occasion. The exploration of the wool fibre, both on the living animal and in the hand, introduced them to a new tactile experience which was related to their clothing. The niceties of the story about straw and clay were much more apparent to them after watching the spinning process, and some of the painting and

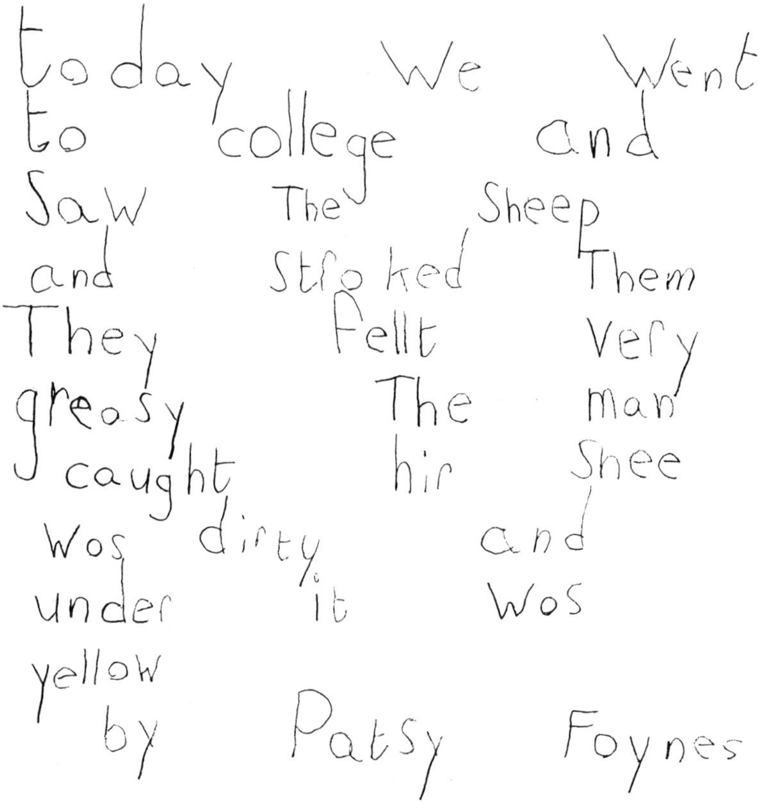

today We Went
to college and
Saw The Sheep
and Stroked Them
They Fellt Very
greasy The man
caught hir Shee
Wos dirty and
under it Wos
yellow
by Patsy Foynes

79 Some writing abo the visit

writing showed a lively observation. The teacher reinforced the occasion by telling the children more about sheep, farming and clothing, and explained how spinning is used in yarn for weaving cloth and for knitting and sewing. They also compiled a chart showing how many children were wearing wool, cotton, etc.

A similar session could take place with slightly older children, the resulting work being appropriate to the age group. Some weaving on simple improvised equipment could be carried out as well. At secondary school level the emphasis could be reversed, with the textile experience forming part of a wider course in any of the appropriate examination subjects such as needlework or domestic science, unless, of course, the study of textiles is being taken at examination level anyway. In that case, the information given throughout this book could form a basis for more advanced techniques.

Museums with textile exhibits (and quite a few have textile collections and examples of primitive looms) could hold sessions in connection with the exhibits. An excellent example of this idea is carried out at the Netherlands Textile Museum at Tilberg where, in addition to the fine collection of looms and textiles, several workshops are run in the evenings and at weekends for children, adults and even the professional weaver. Your local museum, in addition to whatever it has openly on display, may often have interesting textiles which for one reason or another cannot be on public view. Any interested member of the public may ask to see such a collection, and indeed should do so in case it be thought that there is little interest in the subject. The museum provides a vital link with many ancient and foreign textiles.

My final advice is for the beginner. Do not despair, confronted by the work of the more experienced, that you will never reach any sort of standard. Time after time first-year students have been dismayed at the final third-year display, saying that they would never reach that level of achievement; and each year the final work *has* achieved an equivalent standard. So see as much professional work as you can; go to exhibitions of student's work (most art schools and colleges of education have them each year); join a class; collect yarns; subscribe to a magazine; join your local Guild of Weavers; and most important of all, *experiment*. Once you have attempted the first piece of work and conquered the problems, you will gain enough confidence to want to move on. Age, too, is no barrier; my oldest beginner was in her seventies, and I know of many people who start craft activities in middle age. Carry an open mind to your work, never work with material you actively dislike, and be especially open to experiment with new ideas and with colour. Soon you will be able to say, and with pride, 'I made that!'

Some important textile dates

FROM THE FIRST CENTURY AD TO THE PRESENT DAY

1st century	Early writings on textile fibres
2nd century	First cotton in Europe grown in Greece
3rd century	Silk industry developed in Japan
4th century	Silk industry developed in India
552	Silk reached Europe
8th century	First mention of batik, in China
9th century	Silk industry spread to Europe
10th century	Textile Guilds started in Europe and England
11th century	Textile industry grew in Europe and England
12th century	England became an important sheep-producing country due to the settlement of Cistercian monks and the influx of Flemish workers
13th century	England's prosperity based on wool. Many laws passed in connection with the wool trade
14th century	Many more Flemish textile workers settled in England
1492	Columbus discovered cotton in America
1516	Spinning wheel with flyer invented by Leonardo da Vinci; this was never made
1533	Johann Jurgen of Brunswick invented the Saxony wheel, which had a flyer and a treadle. This was the first continuous motion spinning wheel to be used.
1589	William Lee (England) invented the stocking frame
1643	First cotton mill in America
1664	Robert Hooke's *Micrographia* mentioned the possibilities of making an artificial thread
1733	John Kay (England) invented the flying shuttle, which increased the speed of weaving
1767	James Hargreaves (England) invented the Spinning Jenny, which increased the speed of spinning
1769	Richard Arkwright (England) invented a water frame with rollers for spinning
1771	Richard Arkwright became the first mill owner to employ children
1774	Edmund Cartwright (England) invented the power loom
1779	Samuel Crompton (England) invented the mule spinning frame
1785	First use in England of steam power
1792–1801	Joseph-Marie Jacquard (France) invented the Jacquard loom, which lifted groups of thread to produce complex figured designs
1792–4	Eli Whitney (America) invented the cotton gin
1799	First Merino sheep brought to Australia
1823	First power loom in America
1830's	Australia became an important sheep-producing country

1847	The Ten Hour Bill in England prohibited children from working more than ten hours a day
1853	Invention of Perkin's Mauvein by W. H. Perkin (England)
1870	The Education Act in England; child labour ended because education became compulsory
1874	Compulsory education in the USA
1885–9	Artificial silk from mulberry leaves (the forerunner of rayon) first produced by Count Hilaire de Chardonnet in France
1894	Acetate rayon developed in England by Cross, Bevan and Beadle
1895	Viscose rayon developed in England by Cross, Bevan and Beadle
1940	May 15th, first nylon stockings sold in the USA
1955	Reactive dyes developed by I.C.I.

Further reading

Fibres
A Handbook of Textile Fibres by J. Gordon Cook; Merrow Publishing Co, Watford and Textile Book Services. Plainfield, N.J.
Introduction to Fibres and Fabrics by E. Kornreich; Butterworth, London and Elsevier, New York

Yarns and cloth
Practical Macramé by Eugene Andes; Studio Vista, London and Van Nostrand Reinhold, New York
Introducing Macramé by Eirian Short; Batsford, London and Fawcett World Library, New York
Instant Macramé; Graphic Enterprises
The Ashley Book of Knots by C. W. Ashley; Faber, London and Doubleday, New York
Teaching Children Embroidery by Anne Butler; Studio Vista, London
Creative Textile Design: Thread and Fabric by Rolf Hartung; Batsford, London and Van Nostrand Reinhold, New York
Design in Fabric and Thread by Aileen Murray; Studio Vista, London and Watson-Guptill, New York
Designing with String by Mary Seyd; Batsford, London and Watson-Guptill, New York
Dictionary of Embroidery Stitches by Mary Thomas; Hodder & Stoughton, London
The Basic Stitches of Embroidery by Victoria Wade; Victoria and Albert Museum, London and Newbury Books Inc., Boston, Ma.

Weaving
Simple Weaving by Hilary Chetwynd; Studio Vista, London and Watson-Guptill, New York
Your Handweaving by Elsie Davenport; Sylvan Press, London and Select Books, Pacific, Ca.
Off the Loom by Shirley Marein; Studio Vista, London and Viking, New York
Rugweaving for Beginners by Margaret Seagroatt; Studio Vista, London and Watson-Guptill, New York
Weaving is for Anyone by Jean Wilson; Studio Vista, London and Van Nostrand Reinhold, New York
Weaving is Fun by Jean Wilson; Studio Vista, London and Van Nostrand Reinhold, New York

Spinning
Your Handspinning by Elsie Davenport; Sylvan Press, London and Select Books, Pacific, Ca.
Methods of Handspinning in Egypt and the Sudan by Grace M. Crowfoot; Bankfield Museum, Halifax, England

Dyeing and fabric printing
Lichens for Vegetable Dyeing by Eileen Bolton; Studio Vista, London
The Use of Vegetable Dyes by Violetta Thurstan; Dryad Press, Leicester
Vegetable Dyes by Ethel Mairet; Faber, London
Yarn Dyeing by Elsie Davenport; Sylvan Press, London and Select Books, Pacific, Ca.
Dyes and Dyeing by Pat Gilmour; Society for Education through Art, London

Batik for Beginners by Norma Jameson; Studio Vista, London and Watson-Guptill, New York

Tie-and-Dye as a Present Day Craft by Anne Maile; Mills and Boon, London and Taplinger, New York

Tie-and-Dye Made Easy by Anne Maile; Mills and Boon, London

Fun with Fabric Printing by Kathleen Monk; Mills and Boon, London and Textile Book Services, Plainfield, N.J.

Textile Printing and Dyeing by Nora Proud; Batsford, London and Arco, New York

Fabric Printing by Hand by Stephen Russ; Studio Vista, London and Watson-Guptill, New York

History and Museum Publications

Lancashire: the First Industrial Society by C. Aspin; Helmshore Local History Society, Lancashire

Man is a Weaver by E. C. Baity; Harrap, London

The Textile Arts by Verla Birrell; Harrap, London and Schocken Books, New York

Spinning and Weaving by S. E. Ellacott; Methuen, London

Non-European Looms by R. A. Innes; Bankfield Museum, Halifax, England

Ancient Egyptian and Greek Looms by Ling Roth; Bankfield Museum, Halifax, England

History of Dyed Textiles by Stuart Robinson; Studio Vista, London and MIT Press, Cambridge, Ma.

History of Printed Textiles by Stuart Robinson; Studio Vista, London and MIT Press, Cambridge, Ma.

Coptic Weaves by Margaret Seagroatt; Liverpool Museums

Early Decorative Textiles by W. F. Volbach; Hamlyn, London and Textile Book Services, Plainfield, N.J.

Fiction

King Cotton by Thomas Armstrong; Collins, London

The Crowthers of Bankdam by Thomas Armstrong; Collins, London

The Woolpack by Cynthia Harnett; Methuen and Penguin Books, London

UK Suppliers

Dryad, Northgates, Leicester	Spinning, weaving and fabric-dyeing materials and equipment
Dylon International, 139-147 Sydenham Road, London SE26	Dyes in larger quantities
Craftsman's Mark Ltd, Trefnant, Denbigh, N. Wales	Woollen, cotton, hemp and jute yarns
Miss K. R. Drummond, 30 Hart Grove, London W.5	Spinning and weaving equipment and books
A. K. Graupner, Corner House, Valley Road, Bradford 1	Yarns
Multiple Fabric Co. Ltd, Dudley Hill, Bradford 4	Camel, wool and horsehair yarns
Skilbeck Bros. Ltd, 55-7 Glengall Road, London SE15	Direct dyes and acid dyes
Comak Chemicals Ltd, Swinton Works, Moon Street, London N1	Natural and synthetic dyes
Reeves Educational Centre, 178 Kensington High Street, London W8	Reeves Craft Dyes

USA Suppliers

Earth Guild, Inc., 149 Putnam Avenue, Cambridge, Massachusetts	Dyestuffs, mordants, spinning wheels; and fibres (wool, alpaca and others)
The Niddy-Noddy, Croton-on-Hudson, New York	Unusual yarns, weaving and spinning supplies
The Spinster, 34 Hamilton Avenue, Sloatsburg, New York 10974	Unique handspun yarns to order, fibres (fleeces, silk, alpaca, mohair, camel's hair, cashmere, cotton, flax)
Yarn Primitives, P.O. Box 1013, Weston, Connecticut 06880	Imported handspun yarns, including alplaca, goat hair, cotton and others
City Chemical Company, 132 West 22nd Street, New York, New York	Mordants and other chemicals
Brand-Nu Laboratories Inc., P.O. Box 178, Meriden, Connecticut 06450	Natural dyes and chemicals
Clemes & Clemes, 665 San Pablo Avenue, Pinole, California	Spinning wheels; supplies for spinning such as spindles, distaffs, cards

Index